SweetNeedleFelts

25 Projects to Wear, Give and Hug

Jenn Docherty

NORTH LIGHT BOOKS
Cincinnati, Ohio

12 11 10 09 08   5 4 3 2 1

Distributed in Canada by Fraser Direct
100 Armstrong Avenue
Georgetown, ON, Canada L7G 5S4
Tel: (905) 877-4411

Distributed in the U.K. and Europe
by David & Charles
Brunel House, Newton Abbot,
Devon, TQ12 4PU, England
Tel: (+44) 1626 323200, Fax: (+44) 1626 323319
E-mail: postmaster@davidandcharles.co.uk

Distributed in Australia by Capricorn Link
P.O. Box 704, S. Windsor, NSW 2756 Australia
Tel: (02) 4577-3555

Library of Congress Cataloging-in-Publication Data
Docherty, Jenn.
   Sweet needle felts : 25 projects to wear,
give and hug / by Jenn Docherty. -- 1st ed.
      p. cm.
   Includes index.
   ISBN 978-1-60061-039-4 (pbk. : alk. paper)
   1. Felt work. 2. Felting. I. Title.
TT849.5.D625 2008
746'.0463--dc22

2007037793

Editor: Robin M. Hampton
Designer: Maya Drozdz
Production Coordinator: Greg Nock
Photographers: Adam Leigh-Manuell, John Carrico and Adam Henry of Alias Imaging; Tim Grondin; Christine Polomsky
Photo Stylist: Nora Martini

Metric Conversion Chart

to convert	to	multiply by
Inches	Centimeters	2.54
Centimeters	Inches	0.4
Feet	Centimeters	30.5
Centimeters	Feet	0.03
Yards	Meters	0.9
Meters	Yards	1.1
Sq. Inches	Sq. Centimeters	6.45
Sq. Centimeters	Sq. Inches	0.16
Sq. Feet	Sq. Meters	0.09
Sq. Meters	Sq. Feet	10.8
Sq. Yards	Sq. Meters	0.8
Sq. Meters	Sq. Yards	1.2
Pounds	Kilograms	0.45
Kilograms	Pounds	2.2
Ounces	Grams	28.3
Grams	Ounces	0.035

F+W PUBLICATIONS, INC.

www.fwpublications.com

Dedication

To my husband, Jay, and my daughter, Clara...who brighten my every day.

About the Author

Jenn Docherty is a felt artist who makes one-of-a-kind needle-felted creations. Jenn and her needle-felted chicks were recently featured on *The Martha Stewart Show*. After discovering the art of needle felting, Jenn began creating her diminutive creatures and has never looked back. Her work has been featured in various publications and can be found at www.jenndocherty.com.

Acknowledgments

Special thanks to Robin, my lovely editor, and to everyone who made this book a reality! Thank you to my family for putting up with chaos while I needle felt away like a madwoman! Also, thanks to all of the wonderful artists and friends I've met through amazing Internet communities. You've provided such encouragement and inspiration!

Introduction

Fascinating Felt 6

Materials 8

Chapter 1: Techniques 12

Chapter 2: Wearables 22

Flower Pin 24
Woolly Bangle Bracelet 26
Gumdrop Ring 30
Folk Belt 34
Wool and Tulle Winter Hat 36
Strawberry Necklace 38
Woolly Critter T-shirts 42
Free-Form Rose Scarf 44

Chapter 3: For You and Your Home 46

Heart Coasters 48
Crazy for Circles Rug 50
Wispy Pillow 54
Forest Floor Pincushion 58
Birdie Album Cover 62
Fabric Artwork 66
Art Deco Flowers Handbag 68
Woolly Wallet 72
Basket-Weave Bowl 76

Chapter 4: Dolls and Doodads 80

Cute and Cuddly Critters 82
ABC Beanbags 90
Birdie Mobile 92
Catnip Mouse 98
Dog on Wheels 100
Cozy Cottage 104
Fun Fruit 108
Miss Penelope Poppet 110

Templates 116
Resources 124
Index 125

Introduction

Fascinating Felt

I've had a fascination with felt for many years. Alluring in its warmth, texture and versatility, felt is ancient and mysterious, yet modern and fresh at the same time. Traditional felt making utilizes hot, soapy water and hand agitation to bond the wool fibers, transforming them into felt. It's an age-old art that yields amazing results, but it can be a messy, wet business. Needle felting is a fairly new approach to felt making. Special barbed needles originally used in industrial felt making are poked in and out of wool roving, causing the fibers to bond, mat and turn to felt. It's as easy as that. No water, no soap, no mess. It's a completely dry method of felting!

When I first stumbled across the art of needle felting, I immediately knew I could use this technique to bring all of my ideas to life. Needle felting is a process I can use to quickly and neatly embellish, sculpt and make felt fabric from scratch. It's ideal for making jewelry, accessories, cute things for the home and adorable toys—the possibilities are truly endless!

I'd already been successfully working with wet felting to make jewelry and accessories for a number of years before discovering needle felting. However, I began to feel frustrated, because my attempts to create little animals kept failing. Wet felting didn't give me the control over the shapes, so my results simply weren't what I envisioned. When I got my hands on a felting needle, a whole new world of creative possibilities opened up. I began creating one-of-a-kind bears, bunnies and other critters—all from a bit of wool roving! I was able to shape them just the way I wanted them—as though I was sculpting with clay—with tufts of wool and a felting needle. My love of needle felting has evolved into a successful business. My one-of-a-kind critters have homes all over the world, and they've even been featured on *The Martha Stewart Show*.

I'm so happy to be sharing this wonderful technique with you. There's something inherently playful about felt—it's fuzzy and forgiving to work with. The beauty of these projects lies in their simplicity and their fresh approach to needle felting. I designed them paying close attention to color and whimsy. I'm also greatly inspired by the glorious colors of wool roving you can find. Bright colors all heaped into basket are quite a creative thrill. Whatever the reason, I still feel the pull towards fun, colorful designs.

Chapter one will have you mastering the basic skills necessary for needle felting, as well as letting you know exactly what sort of tools you'll need to get started. Chapter two explores the possibilities of felt in the world of wearables with charming accessories to snazz up any outfit or to keep your noggin and neck warm. These cheerful projects are perfect for adorning yourself or for giving as gifts to friends. In chapter three, you'll create personalized items to cozy up every corner of your home. From pillows to wall art to pincushions, fun with felt for you and your home abounds! In chapter four you'll find my favorite things to make with needle felting: whimsical toys, dolls and doodads. These projects explore the sculptural side of needle felting. Make a sweet poppet as a constant companion for your little one. And, the wee animals perched on a shelf are bound to bring a smile.

No matter your skill level or how much time you can devote to crafts, there's a project here for you. I know the projects in this book will have you as excited as I am about the art of needle felting. Happy felting!

Materials

You need only a few basic tools to get started with needle felting. These are readily available from a number of sources, especially now that needle felting is becoming quite popular. Experiment to see what sort of needle, work surface and wool you prefer.

Wool roving and yarn

Wool roving is wool that's been carded and prepared for spinning or felting. There are three main types of wool roving that I like:

*Merino wool is very fine and soft. It's perfect to use for embellishing projects. You can also sculpt with merino, although it's a bit more challenging to work with in this way compared to Corriedale wool.

*Corriedale is a bit coarse and crimpy, but still very soft. It's great to use for embellishing projects as well as for sculpting.

*Romney is best for the beginner to sculpt as it felts very easily and is a very crimpy and coarse fiber.

Wool yarn can be used to add dimension and detail to needle-felted projects.

Foundation fabrics

To embellish with needle felting, you need a foundation fabric on which to work. Whether it's a ready-made item or something you'll be constructing yourself, these fabrics work best:

*Woven wool fabrics, such as those used for apparel, take to needle felting quite well and are available in a range of colors and patterns.

*Wool felt, or felt that has at least 20 percent wool, takes to needle felting nicely. Don't use craft felt: It doesn't contain wool, thus it doesn't accept needle felting very well.

*Recycled wool sweaters are wonderful for needle felting. When tossed into the washer with hot water, they shrink and felt and can then be applied to any number of projects.

*Cottons and linens and other natural fibers accept needle felting.

*Synthetic fabrics are not recommended for needle felting. Your work will peel off because the wool fibers won't bond with the fabric.

Embellishments

There are a variety of embellishments you can apply to your needle-felted projects to personalize them or just to add a bit of sparkle. Beads, sequins, buttons, trim...peruse your local craft store and see what strikes your fancy!

Design-transfer devices

Tracing/transfer paper—Use to transfer designs to fabric.

Cookie cutters and stencils—Use to create crisp shapes on your needle-felted projects.

Marking pen or pencil for fabric—Use to draw directly onto the fabric. Marking pens are available in an air-soluble formula that fades within twenty-four hours.

Chalk—Use to draw designs directly onto your fabric. It also brushes off easily when you're finished.

Felting needles, multineedle tools and shaping tools

Steel felting needles are covered in tiny barbs and come in a variety of sizes. The type of wool you're using and how detailed you want your work to be will determine which needle you use. Felting needles typically come in these sizes:

Size 36: Use this needle to compress the fibers quickly and to felt large pieces quickly. This size is excellent for sculptural pieces.

Size 38: Use this needle to smooth the surface of the wool, to attach the limbs to teddy bears or to appliqué.

Size 40 and 42: Use these needles when you don't want to compress the fibers too much, such as to attach surface embellishments or for detailed work.

Most needles are available with the barbs in either a triangle configuration or a star configuration. The star configuration has more barbs, and therefore felts faster.

I use sizes 36 and 38 in almost all of my work. Try out the different sizes to find your personal preference.

Multineedle holders enable you to work much faster on larger pieces and hold anywhere from two to twenty needles.

Use embroidery hoops, pipe cleaners and skewers to shape your roving and batting.

Use a turning tool to turn narrow tubes of fabric right side out.

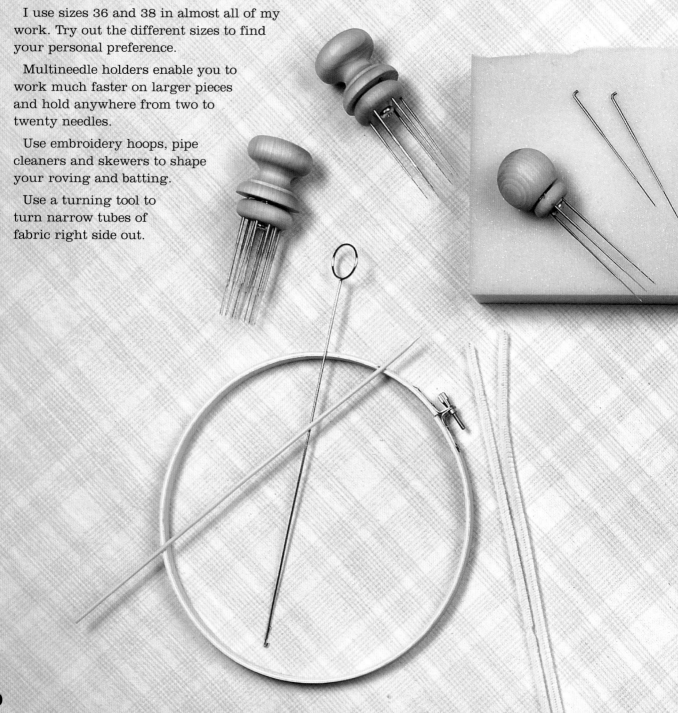

10

Foam work surfaces and forms

Dense foam at least 2" (5cm) thick is an excellent surface to felt on. It gives the needles a soft surface to poke into and prevents your table—or lap—from getting injured.

You can use foam forms to felt around to create shapes, such as those needed for hats, bags and slippers. Once the work is felted, simply remove the felt from the foam form and you have your shape.

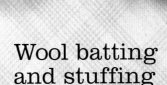

Wool batting and stuffing

Wool batting is wool that has been processed into a sheet of fibers. This is good for working on large projects, such as a rug (page 50). Batting is usually available in natural colors.

Wool stuffing is wool that hasn't been carded and is typically used for stuffing dolls and animals. I use it as a "core" for sculptural projects, as it is less expensive than wool roving.

Sewing notions, jewelry findings and wire

You'll need a few basic supplies for many of the projects in this book—many of which you probably have on hand.

Fabric scissors—straight edge or pinking shears for decorative edges

Needles—sewing, yarn and doll-making

Sewing pins—standard sewing pins to hold fabric together

Thread—sewing and upholstery thread (If you don't have upholstery thread, use unwaxed dental floss!)

Wire, pliers and wire cutters—a fine-gauge wire (projects specify) and jewelry pliers and wire cutters

Jewelry findings—clasps and jump rings

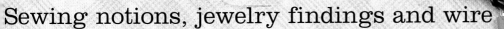

chapter 1

Techniques

A rule to remember with needle felting: There are no rules! (One exception: Safety first when handling those sharp needles.) There are also no complicated techniques that will get in the way of your creativity. Depending on your projects, your work can be as simple or as complex as you desire.

There are three basic areas of technique:

* Surface embellishment: Use this to add pizzazz to any appropriate fabric, clothing or other item.

* Handmade felt fabric: Make your own piece of felt from scratch, then use it in any number of ways, from tiny bags to enormous rugs.

* Sculptural pieces: Sculpt with wool instead of clay to make something as simple as a bead or as wacky as a full-size statue.

Needle Felting

Use this basic technique for all needle-felted surface embellishments you apply to a foundation fabric.

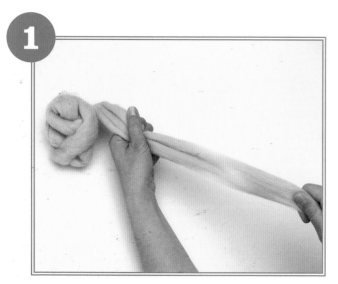

1

Pull wool roving
Hold a rope of wool roving in your hand, and gently tug the wool roving with your other hand to pull off a tuft. Never cut the wool roving.

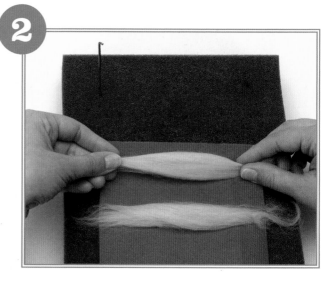

2

Apply wool roving or yarn
Place the foundation fabric on a foam work surface, then lay the tufts of wool roving in an even layer on the foundation fabric.

NEEDLE-FELTING SAFETY

Felting needles are extremely sharp, and you may poke yourself a few times while needle felting. I advise wearing leather finger thimbles or finger protectors (used in quilting) until you feel confident. Here are a few other tips to keep you poke-free:

* Keep your eyes on your work—always! The second you look away to watch something on TV, you'll inevitably poke your finger!

* Jab the needle straight down into your work. Don't bend the needle; it can easily break.

* Work on a stable, flat surface that's not your lap—the needle may poke through your work surface. Buy a small lap desk if you plan on needle felting while sitting on the couch. Place the lap desk on your lap, place your foam work surface on the lap desk, and then you should be safe.

Insert needle
Insert a felting needle into the wool roving and begin to jab the needle in and out through the foundation fabric and down into the foam. Make sure you hold the needle straight.

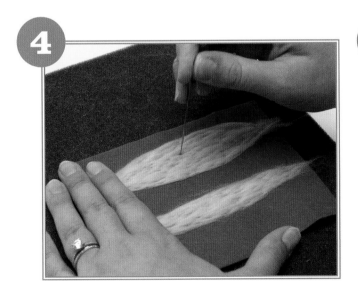

Continue until felted
Continue jabbing the needle in and out until the wool roving fibers have bonded to each other and to the foundation fabric.

Check back of fabric to ensure felting
Flip the fabric or pull up a corner to see if felting is occurring. As the wool roving bonds to the fabric, you'll see the wool roving come through on the other side.

Free-Form Needle Felting

Free-form needle felting enables you to lay wool roving in any pattern or design you desire. This works well for flowing or organic designs where clean, rigid lines aren't necessary.

1

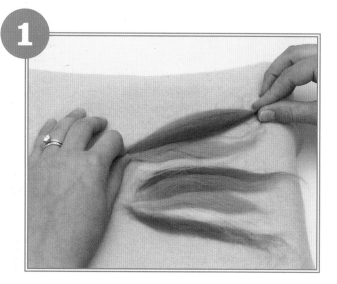

Lay out wool roving or yarn
Form your design by laying out tufts of wool roving in the desired shape on the foundation fabric.

2

Needle felt wool roving or yarn
Needle felt the wool roving or yarn by jabbing the needle down through the wool roving and the fabric. Repeat evenly and consistently until the fibers are bonded and felted to the fabric.

Using a Template

Templates allow you to transfer a design to your fabric and fill it in with needle felting. This works well for complicated or specific designs.

1

Trace template on fabric
Lay the template on the fabric and use a contrasting color pencil or an air-soluble ink pen to trace around the template.

2

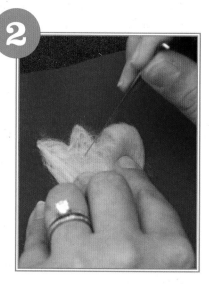

Fill traced area with wool roving
Lay wool roving over the traced design on the fabric, and loosely shape the wool roving to fit in the traced design. Needle felt the wool roving to create the traced shape.

3

Detail edges
Needle felt around the edge of the shape to assure crisp outlines.

Transferring a Pattern

Transfer (tracing) paper made for transferring designs to fabric is an ideal way of copying your artwork or a template onto your foundation fabric.

1

2

3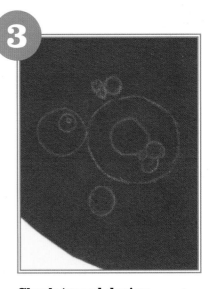

Lay transfer paper on fabric
Place transfer paper on top of the fabric. Be sure the fabric is on a hard surface (not foam), and be sure the transfer side of the paper is facing the fabric.

Trace design
Lay the design on top of the transfer paper. Using a writing utensil or a stylus, apply pressure while tracing the design.

Check traced design
Remove the design template and the transfer paper from the fabric.

Using a Stencil or a Cookie Cutter

Stencils and cookie cutters are great for achieving crisp, simple needle-felted shapes. The needle stays within the confines of a cookie cutter, so this is an excellent way for a beginner to protect her fingers. Using stencils or cookie cutters is also a great way to introduce needle felting to an older child.

1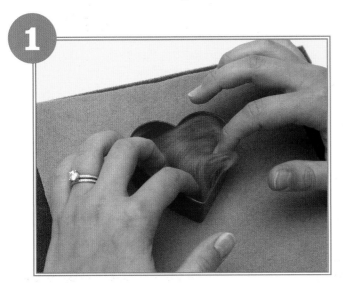

2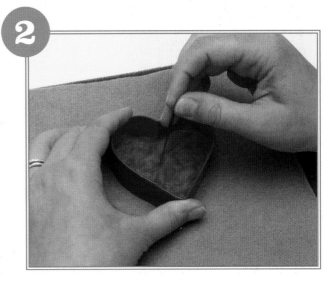

Fill stencil or cookie cutter
Place a stencil or cookie cutter on the fabric, over a foam work surface. Fill the shape with wool roving.

Needle felt wool roving
Keep the stencil or cookie cutter in place and needle felt the wool roving until you've filled the shape with the desired thickness of felted wool roving.

Adding Yarn for Dimension

Beautiful wool yarns can add twirly, swirly dimension and lovely details to your needle felting.

Design with yarn

Create your own masterpiece by laying yarn onto fabric (over a foam work surface) to create a design, needle felting as you go.

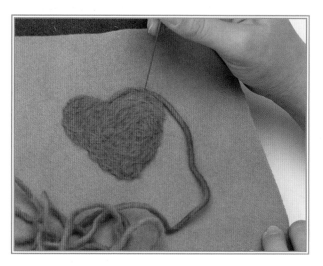

Outline with yarn

Lay yarn around the edges of your needle-felted designs; needle felt as you go to create dramatic outlines.

Needle Felting Wool Appliqués

Commercial wool felt can be cut into shapes and then needle felted onto a foundation fabric. This creates stitch-less appliqués that meld seamlessly with fabric. (For this application, use wool felt, not synthetic craft felt.)

Cut design from felt

Cut around a template (or trace the template first) or cut a free-form shape from wool felt.

Needle felt appliqué to fabric

Lay the appliqué on fabric and needle felt until the piece fuses to the fabric.

Making Felt Fabric

You can create felt fabric by hand. Once you've created felt fabric, use it for any number of projects or let it stand alone as a piece of art.

1

Lay out wool roving

Lay tufts of wool roving horizontally directly on a foam work surface. Lay an even layer of tufts vertically on top of the horizontal tufts.

2

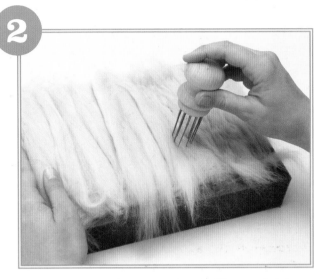

Needle felt wool roving together

Use a multineedle tool to needle felt the layers of wool roving until they're bonded together.

3

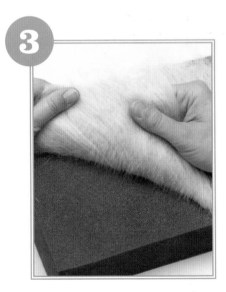

Flip fabric

Peel the partially felted fabric off the foam. Flip the fabric over and place it on the foam.

4

Continue needle felting and flipping

Fold over any wispy ends and needle felt them in place to create a clean edge. Repeat steps 2 and 3 until you have a firmly bonded piece of felt fabric.

Use cookie cutters to create shapes

To make shaped fabric, fill a cookie cutter with wool roving, then follow steps 2–4.

Creating Balls or Beads from Wool Roving

There are many uses for felt balls or beads. This most basic sculptural technique can be used for beads of any size.

1

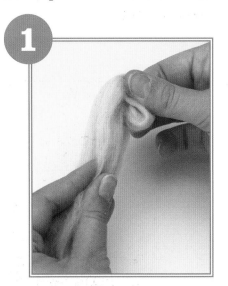

2

3

Form ball

Roll a tuft of wool roving between your fingers to form a ball that's about twice the size you would like your finished ball or bead to be.

Needle felt and shape ball

Place the ball on your foam work surface. Jab the felting needle in and out, turning the wool roving as you go to form a round ball.

Flatten sides as needed.

When the ball is firm and of the desired size, press it onto a hard, flat surface and roll the ball back and forth to flatten it into shape. Needle felt along the flat side to strengthen the shape.

Creating a Core

Using a core ensures that your projects will be firm. To make the most of your craft budget, create cores from wool stuffing—it's less expensive than wool roving.

1

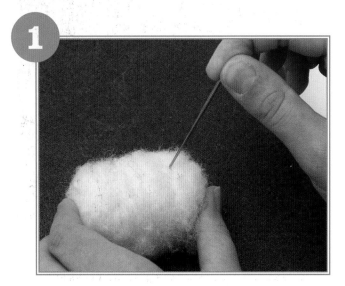

2

Form a core with wool stuffing

Roll a handful of wool stuffing into a ball and needle felt it until it's moderately firm. It should be about three-quarters the size of the desired finished shape.

Cover core with wool roving

Wrap wool roving around the core and needle felt it in place until it's smooth, secure and nicely felted.

Shaping with Skewers

Wrapping wool roving around a wooden skewer is an easy way to create oblong or oval shapes. This technique allows you to control the firmness and shape of your wool. You can create core shapes with stuffing; for smaller pieces, simply wrap the wool roving itself around the skewer.

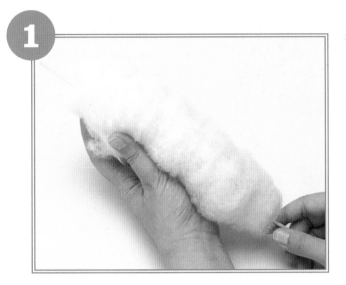

1

Create core with wool stuffing
Pull a tuft of wool stuffing twice as large as the desired finished shape. Wrap the wool stuffing tightly around the skewer to shape it. Slide the wool stuffing off the skewer.

2

Needle felt core to desired shape
Needle felt the stuffing into the desired shape. Continue to needle felt until the fibers have bonded together.

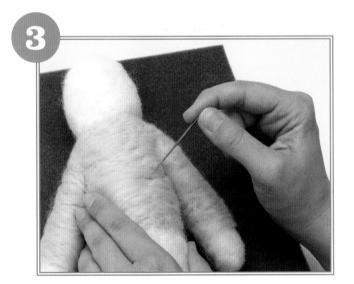

3

Apply wool roving to core
Wrap wool roving around the core to cover it. Needle felt the wool roving in place until it's smooth and secure and nicely felted.

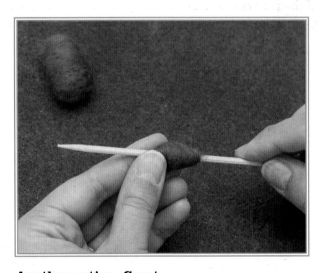

Another option: Create shapes with wool roving
Wrap a small tuft of wool roving around a wooden skewer. Remove the wool roving from the skewer, then needle felt it until it's firm. Taper an end as you go.

Needle Felting onto Foam Forms

Foam forms are available for needle felting hats, purses and even slippers. These forms can be adapted for other projects as well. You can also cut out your own foam shapes and cover them with wool roving to create a core for your sculptural pieces.

1

Apply wool roving
Lay wool roving on a foam form. Needle felt the wool roving to the form.

2

Create layers
You can add a second layer of wool roving in the opposite direction to strengthen or create thickness, if desired.

3

Flip and needle felt other side
When using the foam form to structure the shape, remove the felted wool roving, flip or turn it inside out and replace the felted wool roving on the foam form. Continue to needle felt. Repeat turning and needle felting until the desired consistency is achieved.

FUN TIP

You don't have to remove the felt from the foam form; you can use the foam form to add stability to your project. See the *Cozy Cottage* (page 104) to see how foam can give you a squeezable foundation.

Creating an Armature

Armatures provide stability, poseability and a flexible foundation for sculptural pieces.

Twist pipe cleaners together
Twist the pipe cleaners together to form the basic shape. (Wool roving adheres better to pipe cleaners than wire.)

Shape skeleton
Bend the pipe cleaners to form the desired shape.

Apply wool roving to armature
Wrap wool roving in the desired shape around the pipe-cleaner skeleton until you have almost twice the size of the desired finished project.

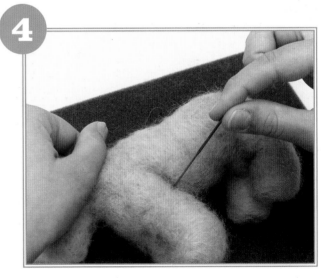

Needle felt wool roving
Needle felt the wool roving until it's firmly bonded and the desired shape and size are reached.

chapter **2**

Wearables

The textures and colors of wool are perfect for creating fresh wearable items, which you can add to your own wardrobe or give as gifts. Most of the projects in this chapter are quick and easy, perfect for whipping up in just a few hours before you dash out the door. They definitely give a fun, colorful bit of flair to an otherwise regular old wardrobe.

Add a sweet and colorful touch to sweaters or jackets with the charming *Flower Pin* (page 24). If you're feeling a little more on the fun and funky side, try the *Woolly Bangle Bracelet* (page 26) or the *Gumdrop Ring* (page 30). If you need a last-minute gift, take a look at the *Free-Form Rose Scarf* (page 44) or the *Woolly Critter T-shirts* (page 42) for the smaller set!

Flower Pin

Lovely woolen petals come together to form a colorful bloom that's particularly nice pinned to a coat or a purse.

MATERIALS

* Wool roving—olive green and pink
* Scrap of fabric or felt—green
* Pin back
* Fabric glue
* Felting needle
* Foam work surface

Form petals

Pull 3 equal-sized—approximately 6" (15cm)—tufts of pink wool roving for the outer petals. Pull 3 slightly smaller equal-sized pieces for the inner petals. To form a petal, fold a tuft of the pink wool roving in half, lay it flat on the foam work surface, and needle felt the petal shape. You can use my template as a guide (page 116). The fold will be the top of the petal.

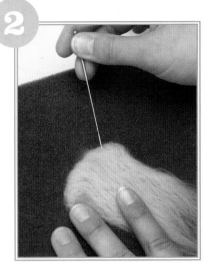

Shape petals

To shape a petal, needle felt perpendicularly along the outside edge. Watch your fingers! Leave wispy ends at the bottom of the petal—don't needle felt. Repeat with the remaining tufts to form 6 petals.

Join petals

Lay out the petals with the wispy ends overlapping at the center of the flower. Needle felt the middle of the flower to join the petals.

Form center

Pull a large tuft of olive green wool roving and wind it into a ball. Needle felt the ball onto the middle of the flower, first inserting the needle straight through the middle of the ball, then shaping and securing the ball along its outside edge.

Attach pin back

Attach a pin back to the back of the flower with a strong fabric glue. Glue a small scrap of green felt or fabric over the base of the pin back—not over the pin—or needle felt some wool roving over the base of the pin back.

FUN IDEAS

* Try different shapes, quantities or sizes of petals!

* Of course you can always embellish your flower!

Woolly Bangle Bracelet

This bracelet has a very modern feel. Don't get hung up trying to make it perfect. It looks great when it's a bit messy!

MATERIALS

* Wool roving—dark turquoise and lime green
* Thread—2 or more colors
* Felting needle
* Foam work surface
* Sewing machine

Lay out wool roving

Lay a tuft of dark turquoise wool roving, approximately 1" x 10" (3cm x 25cm) horizontally on your foam work surface. Lay smaller tufts vertically on top of the horizontal tufts. [It's OK for these to be quite a bit longer than 1" (3cm); you'll incorporate these "loose ends" later.]

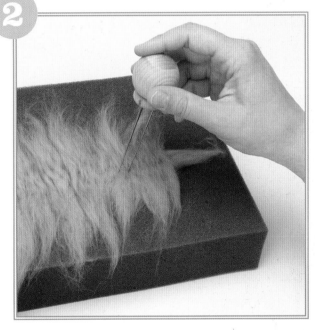

Needle felt center

Begin needle felting, concentrating your efforts on the middle portion of each vertical tuft, leaving overhanging wispy edges.

TIP

When pulling the wool roving, make sure it completely circles your wrist—and then pull it a little longer. The size of the wool roving will decrease as the fibers are bonded.

Before proceeding to step 3, make sure
the bracelet wraps comfortably around
your wrist. If it doesn't, needle felt more
roving horizontally, extending the length
of the bracelet

TIP

3

Flip, then needle felt other side

Carefully peel the wool roving off the foam
work surface. Turn the wool roving over, fold-
ing vertical wisps over onto the horizontal
fibers to create an even edge. Needle felt the
vertical fibers in place, smoothing the edges
with the needle as you go. Flip the piece over
and needle felt the other side. Continue flipping and needle felting until you achieve the
desired texture.

4

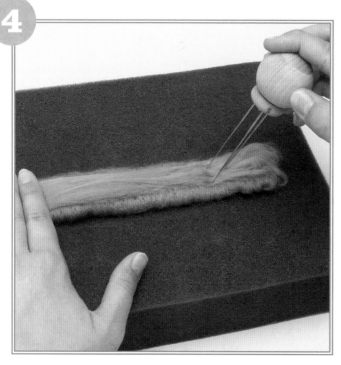

Apply contrasting wool roving

Lay the lime green wool roving horizontally
through the middle of the bracelet. Needle
felt this strip in place.

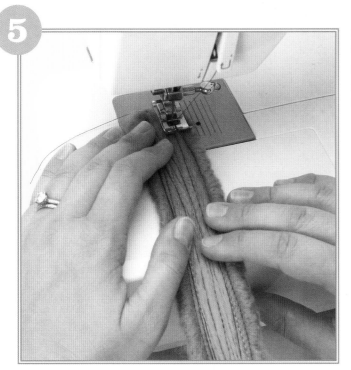

Sew design with thread

With a sewing machine, stitch various colors of thread lengthwise on the bracelet. The thread stripes don't need to be neat or straight.

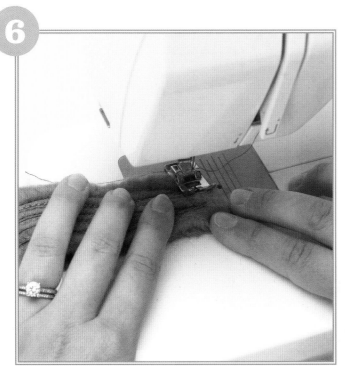

Join ends

Fold the bracelet in half wrong-side out (the lime green strip doesn't show), and stitch the ends together. Go back and forth a few times to secure the seam. Run a zigzag stitch to cover the seam. Turn the piece right-side out, and wear your funky and unique wool bangle proudly!

Gumdrop Ring

Colorful and bold, this ring is sure to garner attention! You can make one to match your every mood.

MATERIALS

* Wool roving—light blue
* Small tufts of wool roving— olive green, red and white
* Ring base with flat pad to hold embellishment
* Seed beads
* Thread
* Felting needle
* Sewing needle with eye that fits through seed bead
* Foam work surface
* Strong fabric glue
* Scissors

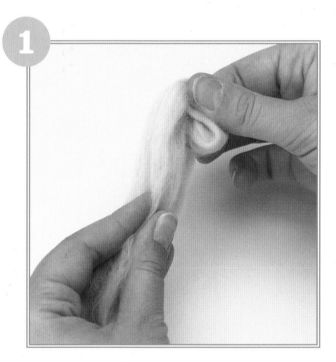

1

Shape wool roving into ball

Roll a tuft of light blue wool roving between your fingers to form a ball. Start with a ball about twice the size you would like your finished gumdrop to be.

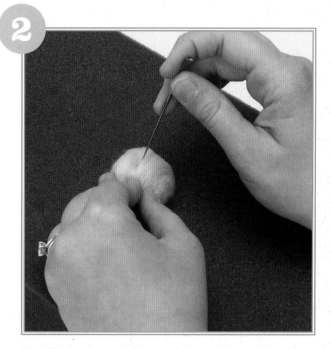

2

Needle felt and shape ring

Place the ball of wool roving on your foam work surface and begin jabbing the felting needle in and out, turning the wool roving as you go to form a round ball.

FUN IDEAS

* **Make different sizes—Why not a jumbo ring or pendant?**

* **Jazz up your gumdrops with sequins!**

Create flat side

When the ball of wool roving is firm and has shrunk to about half of its original size, press it onto a hard, flat surface and roll it back and forth to flatten a side and achieve the gum-drop shape. Needle felt along the flat side to strengthen the shape.

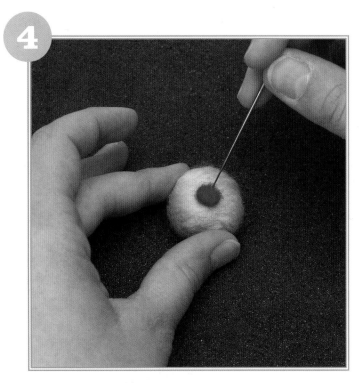

Create and apply polka dots

Roll tiny tufts of red wool roving between your fingers to form small balls. Needle felt each small ball onto the gumdrop to create polka dots. Repeat with olive green and white wool roving, if desired.

5

Stitch on beads

To attach the seed beads, first thread your sewing needle and knot the thread at the end. Push the sewing needle through the middle of the bottom of the gumdrop and out through a polka dot. Thread a seed bead onto the needle, and push the bead down against the gumdrop. Insert the sewing needle back into the polka dot and against the bead to secure the bead, and exit through the next spot you wish a bead to be placed. Continue sewing beads onto the polka dots, and when you are finished adding beads, exit through the bottom of the gumdrop and tie off the thread. Snip the excess thread.

6

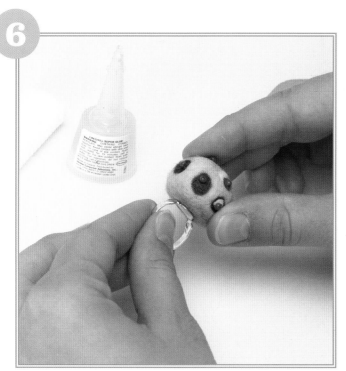

Glue gumdrop to ring

Apply strong fabric glue to the ring base and place the gumdrop on the glued base. Hold the gumdrop in place until the glue is set.

FUN IDEA

Try making a pendant or a pin, as well! Purchase pendant and pin bases with flat pads that will hold your creations.

Folk Belt

This belt was inspired by milkmaids and old-fashioned Dutch girls in clogs. It's meant to be worn high on the waist, around a T-shirt or a sweet dress. This belt is the perfect way to add a colorful, fun flair to an otherwise boring outfit.

Of course, if the folksy feel isn't your style, you could simplify or modernize this belt very easily by omitting the rickrack and using clean, geometric shapes.

MATERIALS

* Wool felt—red, ⅛ yard (11cm) of 36" (91cm) width fabric
* Small scraps of wool felt—light blue, olive green and pink
* Small tuft of wool roving—white
* Rickrack—white
* Fabric glue
* Felting needle
* Foam work surface
* Scissors

1

Cut pieces from felt

Cut the belt shape from the red wool felt using a template (page 117). Cut 1 tulip from the light blue wool felt, 2 hearts from the pink wool felt and 2 leaves from the olive green wool felt.

2

Needle felt appliqués to belt

Lay the belt on the foam work surface and place the tulip appliqué in the middle of the belt. Needle felt the tulip in place; start by securing the middle of the tulip, and then concentrate on the outside edges to maintain integrity of the shape. Needle felt 1 heart on both sides of the tulip and 2 leaves under the tulip.

3

Add flower embellishments

Needle felt 2 dots of white wool roving over the tulip.

4

Add rickrack

Use fabric glue to attach the rickrack around the needle-felted design. Extend a length of the rickrack down each side and glue it in place, ensuring that you leave enough length to tie around your waist.

TIP

It's easy to adjust the belt's length to fit. Measure around your waist and determine where you would like the red felt portion of the belt to end, and adjust your rickrack accordingly to tie in the back to fit. It's a very simple and versatile pattern that can be easily altered.

FUN IDEAS

* Try experimenting with colors and shapes. Add a scalloped edge, perhaps.

* Use ribbon for the ties. Velvet or silk would also be lovely.

* Combine stitching and embellishments with your felting.

Wool and Tulle Winter Hat

Winter wear can be rather dull. When you're already feeling blue from the cold, why not warm things up a bit by adorning a plain old hat you may have lying around? Tulle blossoms add a bit of fun to this basic red hat. Needle felting a ball of wool roving directly into the center of a flower to attach it to the hat makes this project glue free, sewing free, and virtually pain free. Just watch out for those needles!

MATERIALS

* Wool roving—olive green
* Small tufts of wool roving—orange and white
* Tulle—orange, pink and white
* Wool winter hat
* Felting needle
* Foam work surface
* Pinking shears

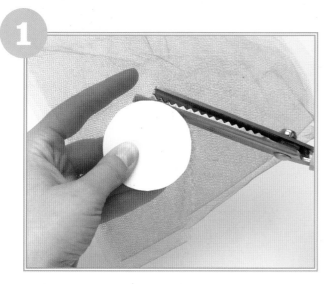

1

Cut tulle flowers

Fold a piece of pink tulle into a 4-layer square. Use your pinking shears to cut a circle 2" (5cm) in diameter to create a layered "blossom." Repeat with the white and orange tulle to make 2 more blossoms.

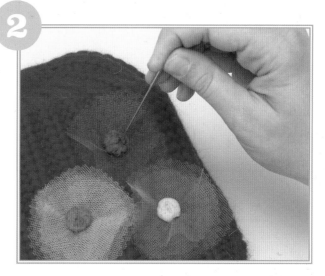

2

Needle felt centers

Stretch a hat over a foam work surface. To attach the tulle circles to the hat, keep each "blossom" in a stack of 4 circles. Lay the first circle on the hat, and needle felt a tuft of wool roving to the center of the circle; jab through both the tulle and the hat. Keep needle felting until the blossom is firmly attached to hat. Repeat this step 2 times to attach the other tulle blossoms.

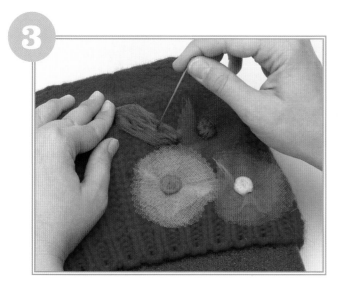

3

Add leaves

Lay a tuft of the olive green wool roving on the hat in the spot where you wish to add a leaf. Needle felt the wool roving into a leaf shape, using the felting needle to manipulate the shape as you go.

FUN IDEAS

* You can also use cotton fabric to make the blossoms. While the pinking shears slow down fraying, you can use a bit of fray blocker to further prevent the edges from fraying. You can skip the fray blocker and let them fray for a fun look, too.

* Try this embellishment to liven up an old sweater.

Strawberry Necklace

Sweet felt strawberries can be a whimsical addition to your jewelry box. This necklace is perfect for big girls and little girls alike!

MATERIALS

* Wool roving—dark turquoise, olive green, pink and red
* Silk beading cord—red [approximately 30" (76cm) for a 17" (43cm) necklace]
* Seed beads—red and Kelly green
* 2 clamshell knot covers
* Strong fabric glue
* Thread to match seed beads
* Felting needle
* Foam work surface
* Thick, sharp sewing needle
* Pliers

1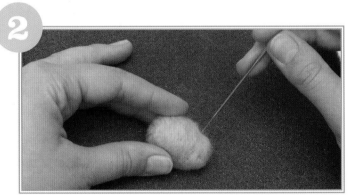

Create beads

Pull equal-sized tufts of dark turquoise and olive green wool roving, 1 tuft for each bead you want to make— I chose to make 12. Wind a tuft of wool roving into a ball and needle felt it; turn it as you go to ensure you achieve an even round shape. Repeat for each tuft of wool roving.

2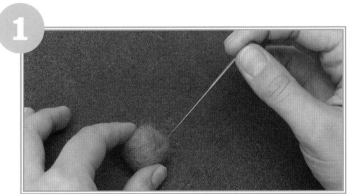

Create strawberries

To make a strawberry, roll a tuft of pink wool roving into a tight ball, about the size of a golf ball. Needle felt the wool roving, turning it as you go. As the ball starts to form, focus your needle felting on an end to taper and form the strawberry shape. Repeat this step for each strawberry—I made 2 pink and 1 red.

3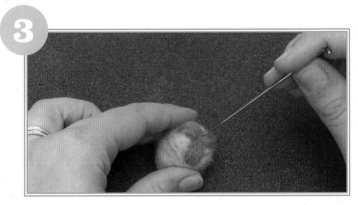

Make strawberry leaves

Roll a small tuft of olive green wool roving between your fingers to form a small snake shape about 1" (3cm) long. Repeat twice for 3 leaves total. Join the middle of the 3 leaves at the top of a strawberry. Needle felt each leaf down the side of the strawberry; shape with a felting needle as you go. Repeat for the remaining strawberries.

4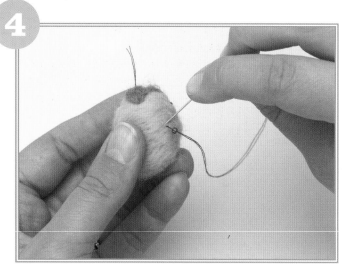

Add strawberry "seeds"

Thread a sewing needle with a thread that matches the bead color and tie a knot in the end. I used red seed beads on the pink strawberries and green seed beads on the red strawberry. Push the needle into the top of the strawberry, and pull the knot to secure it. Thread a seed bead onto the needle and thread, and push the bead down against the strawberry. Insert the sewing needle back into the strawberry against the bead to secure the bead, and exit through the next place on the strawberry where you want to attach a seed. Continue attaching seed beads. After the last bead, exit through the top of the strawberry and tie a knot in the thread to finish. Bury any thread that remains under a small tuft of wool roving. Repeat this step for each strawberry.

5

Lay out felt beads and strawberries

Lay out your felt beads and strawberries in the design you want—I placed the strawberries in the middle and alternated the turquoise and green felt beads with 6 on each side. Cut the silk beading cord in a length that's workable yet longer than the layout of your felt pieces.

6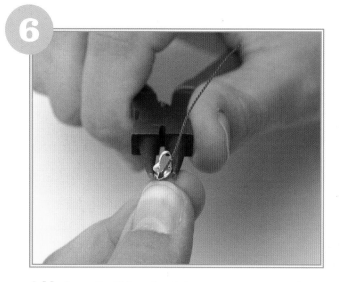

Add clamshell knot cover

Tie a knot in the end of the silk cord. Thread on a clamshell knot cover. Put a drop of glue on the knot and use pliers to close the knot cover over the knot.

7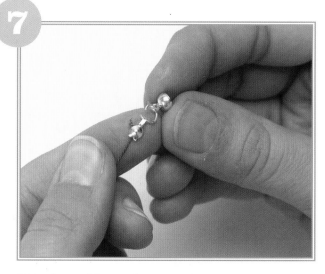

Attach necklace closure

Attach one-half of the necklace closure to the loop on the knot cover. Use pliers to close the jump ring.

8

Thread seed beads, felt beads and strawberries on cord

Thread 4 seed beads—I used red seed beads—onto the silk cord. Use your large sewing needle to thread on a felt ball and 4 seed beads. Follow your pattern from step 5, alternating 4 seed beads with the felt balls and strawberries. End with 4 seed beads.

9

Create second closure

Thread the other clamshell knot cover onto the cord against the last seed bead. Tie a knot very close to the knot cover. Put a dab of glue on the knot, and use pliers to close the cover over the knot. Trim the excess cord. Attach the rest of the necklace closure to the knot cover as in step 7. Your felt strawberry necklace is complete!

FUN IDEAS

* Make your necklace a long, flapper style. Use multiple colors and shapes for the beads—you can even combine ceramic, glass or wooden beads with your felt ones!

* Try different fruits! Cherries would be fun, as would oranges, lemons and limes.

* Make a bracelet to match.

Woolly Critter T-shirts

This is a fun way to adorn a child's T-shirt, and it's perfect for covering those unsightly stains!

Do you need cookie cutters? Look online to discover hundreds of shapes. The possibilities are endless for creating great designs. You might just want to make a few T-shirts for yourself!

Experiment with multiple colors of wool roving in one design, or keep it super simple, as shown here.

MATERIALS

* Wool roving—purple
* Small tuft of wool roving—white
* Cotton T-shirt
* Cookie cutter in animal shape
* Felting needle
* Foam work surface
* Air-soluble fabric marking pen

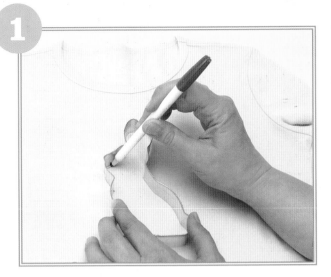

Trace design

Lay the T-shirt flat and place a cookie cutter in the center. Mark the design with an air-soluble marking pen for fabric.

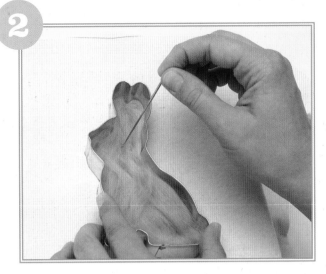

Needle felt wool roving

Stretch the marked T-shirt over a foam work surface and lay the cookie cutter on top of the marked outline. Fill the cookie cutter with an even layer of purple wool roving. Begin needle felting—pay careful attention to the edges to ensure a clear design. Continue until the wool roving is smooth and firmly felted.

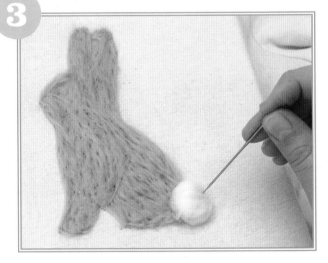

Add embellishments

Roll a small tuft of white wool roving in your hand to form a small ball. Needle felt the ball to attach the tail to the bunny.

TIPS

Wash in cold water on the gentle cycle. Smooth the design as needed by gently ironing it with the iron on wool setting. Cover the design with a pressing cloth and use light steam.

FUN IDEAS

* Embellish, embellish, embellish! Why not stitch on beads, button, or sequins.

* Make different designs for all ages. Onesies for baby would be darling!

* Try this technique on cotton pants, bags or place mats. Go crazy!

Free-Form Rose Scarf

If knitting isn't your thing, then this is the scarf for you! Wool fabric and a bit of wool yarn are all you need to make this pretty scarf. This also makes a quick and easy gift!

MATERIALS

* Wool yarn—light turquoise and hot pink
* Wool fabric—red, ¼–½ yard (23–46cm) of 60" (152cm) width
* Felting needle
* Foam work surface
* Yarn needle
* Fabric scissors
* Air-soluble fabric marking pen
* Tape measure or ruler

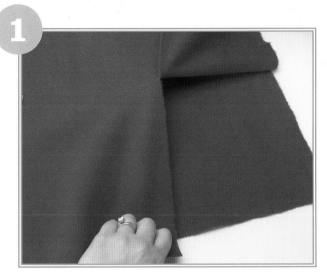

1

Mark and tear fabric

Mark the measurements for the scarf on the wool fabric. If your fabric is woven wool, you can make a snip with your scissors and then tear the length of the fabric. This gives you a perfect, even tear with a fringed edge. If you're using commercial wool felt fabric, tearing it won't work. Instead, cut your fabric. My scarf measures 7¼" × 60" (18cm × 152cm). I let the width of the wool determine the length of the scarf.

2

Create fringed edge

Pull the thread around the remaining edges to create a fringe. This should hold well; however, you can run a stitch around the scarf to keep the edges from unraveling.

3

Add flower embellishment

Cut a long length of light turquoise wool yarn. Place the scarf on a foam work surface, and place the end of the wool yarn where you want the center of the rose to be. Needle felt the end of the yarn in place. Spiral the yarn in a wavy fashion to represent petals. Tack the yarn in place with a felting needle as you go. After you've finished laying out the rose, needle felt it securely in place. Repeat this step for as many roses as you wish to make. Add leaves with the hot pink wool yarn in the same manner.

4

Add fringe

For the fringe, snip several 8" (20cm) lengths of the light turquoise wool yarn. The number of pieces you need will depend on the type of yarn you use and the width of your scarf. Thread both ends of yarn through the eye of the yarn needle, through the top side of scarf about ¼" (6mm) from the bottom edge. Be sure to leave the loop on the top side. Guide the needle with the yarn ends through the loop and pull the yarn ends to secure. Repeat! Voilà! You have your fringe.

chapter 3

For You and Your Home

The warmth of wool lends itself perfectly to cozy and unique accessories for you and your home. Wool brings depth and tactility to any corner of your home. From livening up a simple pillow to creating an entire rug, you can add a fuzzy, textural touch to your world with these unique projects!

The *Heart Coasters* (page 48) are a perfect resting spot for a cup of cocoa in front of the hearth! Adorn your walls with a super simple technique for creating a woolly masterpiece with the *Fabric Artwork* (page 66). When you're ready to head out on the town, take some of the warmth of home with you by carrying the *Art Deco Flowers Handbag* (page 68) and stash your dough in your *Woolly Wallet* (page 72).

Heart Coasters

This is a sweet and simple project, which enlists the help of cookie cutters to achieve uniform and crisp shapes. This is a great project for beginners, as the cookie cutters help keep the needles away from fingers!

MATERIALS

* Wool roving—dark turquoise, olive green and pink
* Round cookie cutter—3½" (9cm) in diameter
* Heart cookie cutter—smaller than the round cookie cutter
* Felting needle(s)
* Foam work surface
* Multineedle tool (optional)

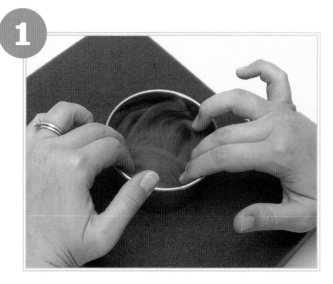

Place wool roving in cookie cutter

Place the round cookie cutter on a foam work surface. Arrange an even layer of the olive green wool roving inside the round cookie cutter. Add another layer of the olive green wool roving with the fibers running in the opposite direction.

Needle felt wool roving into fabric

Begin needle felting—a multineedle tool makes this go faster. Pay careful attention to the edges for a crisp shape.

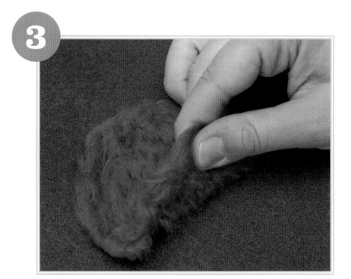

Flip and needle felt other side

Gently peel the coaster from the foam work surface. Flip the coaster over and place it back inside cookie cutter. Needle felt this side. Continue to flip and needle felt until the coaster base is fully felted. Set the round cookie cutter aside. Keep the coaster on the foam work surface.

Add heart to coaster

Place a heart cookie cutter on top of the coaster. Arrange an even layer of the dark turquoise wool roving inside the heart cookie cutter. Needle felt the roving to secure the heart to the coaster base. Pay careful attention to the edges for a crisp shape.

Crazy for Circles Rug

In case you haven't noticed already, I love circles and dots! This rug takes the technique of using a cookie cutter to achieve perfect circles and blows it up to a large scale. Using embroidery hoops, available at craft stores, you can create a soft 100 percent wool rug. Get ambitious! This is a small throw rug, but with enough wool you could make a larger area rug.

MATERIALS

* Wool roving—pink and red
* Wool batting—charcoal
* Small scraps of felt—red
* Flower cookie cutters
* Round cookie cutter—3½" (9cm) in diameter
* Embroidery hoop—8" (20cm) in diameter
* Multineedle tool
* Large foam work surface
* Scissors
* Fabric glue

1

Create felt circles

Placed an embroidery hoop on a foam work surface. Lay 2 layers of the charcoal wool batting inside the embroidery hoop. Use a multineedle tool to needle felt the batting until the fibers begin to bond. Pay careful attention to the edges to maintain the integrity of the circle.

2

Flip and needle felt other side

Peel the wool circle off the foam work surface, flip the circle over and place it back inside the embroidery hoop. Needle felt this side. Continue to flip and needle felt until the circle is firmly felted; keep the circle within the hoop to achieve a nice shape. When you flip the wool circle feel for any thin, weak spots and add more wool batting as needed. Repeat steps 1–2 to make more large circles. (I made 6 large circles for this small throw rug.)

TIP

This project uses wool batting in addition to wool roving. Batting comes in large rolls. This is basically the same as wool roving, but batting enables you to lay out sheets of wool, as opposed to small tufts. Featured here is a Corriedale batting in charcoal; it's also available in colors. When planning your rug, consider how large you want your rug to be and how much you want to spend. Some types of batting are more expensive than others.

Create filler circles

Repeat steps 1–2 to make 2 small circles. Use the round cookie cutter instead of the embroidery hoop, and use the red wool roving instead of the wool batting.

Add embellishments

Place one of the large felt circles on a foam work surface. Lay the flower cookie cutter on top of one of the large felt circles. Fill the flower cookie cutter with the pink wool roving and needle felt to adhere the wool roving to the felt circle.

Join circles to form rug

Cut small strips from the red wool felt scraps and glue 1 strip in each spot where 2 circles meet. Allow the glue to dry, and turn the rug face up. Instead of gluing the strips on, you can use strong thread to stitch the circles together on the rug's underside. However, given the scale, this may be time consuming.

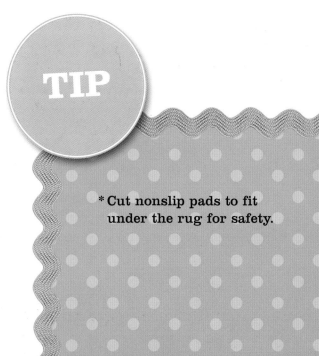

TIP

* Cut nonslip pads to fit under the rug for safety.

variation * Circle Trivet

MATERIALS

* Wool roving
* Round cookie cutters in different sizes
* Thread
* Multineedle tool
* Large foam work surface
* Sewing needle
* Scissors

1

Create circles

Use various sizes of round cookie cutters and follow steps 1–3 from the rug project to create multiple circles in varying colors.

2

Join circles with thread

Use heavy thread to stitch the circles together on what will be the underside of the trivet. This piece is perfect for the dinner table!

FUN IDEAS

* Use huge embroidery hoops to make gigantic circles. Vary your circle sizes to create a more free-form, abstract rug (like the trivet, but larger).

* If you want to use items you have on hand, search the house for circular, tubelike objects (oatmeal containers, pie tins) to use as circle templates. Just cut the item in half or cut out the bottom, and needle felt away!

Wispy Pillow

Combine simple techniques with vibrant wool roving to create a one-of-a-kind accessory sure to brighten your décor. Think of the possibilities: throw pillows, sachets, and door or wall hangings that are simple enough to whip up in minutes.

MATERIALS

* Wool roving—dark turquoise, light turquoise, lime green, olive green and orange
* Wool fabric—pink, ½ yard (46cm)
* Cotton fabric—½ yard (46cm)
* Wool felt—orange
* Wool yarn—brown
* Polyester filling
* Thread
* Felting needle
* Foam work surface
* Sewing needle
* Fabric scissors
* Tape measure
* Straight pins
* Sewing machine (optional)

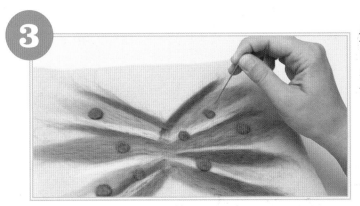

1. Cut wool and cotton fabric
Cut a 15½" x 10" (39cm x 25cm) piece of wool fabric for the front of the pillow and a 15½" x 10" (39cm x 25cm) piece of cotton fabric for the back of the pillow.

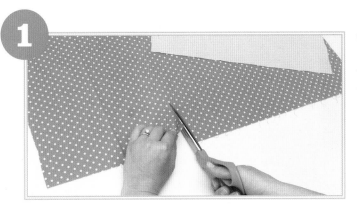

2. Lay out wool roving in wing pattern
Lay the wool fabric on a foam work surface. Pull wisps of the dark turquoise, light turquoise, lime green and olive green wool roving. Lay out wisps in a wing configuration, so they meet in the middle and fan toward the sides.

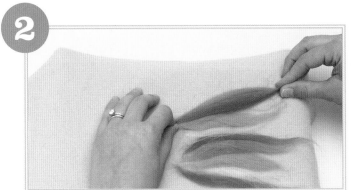

3. Needle felt wings and embellishments
Needle felt the wisps of wool roving in place. Roll small tufts of orange wool roving into balls. Needle felt the randomly placed dots onto the wings.

4

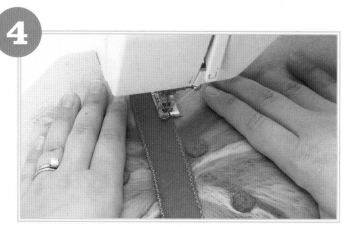

Sew moth body to pillow

Cut the moth body from wool felt using the template (page 118). Pin the orange felt in place, in the center of the wings. Use thread in a contrasting color to zigzag stitch around the outside edge of the body. (If you don't have a sewing machine, glue the body in place using fabric glue, or hand stitch around edge of the body.)

5

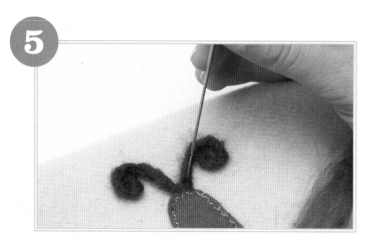

Create antennae with yarn

Needle felt 2 small lengths of brown wool yarn from the top of the body. Spiral the end of each piece of yarn to form the antennae.

6

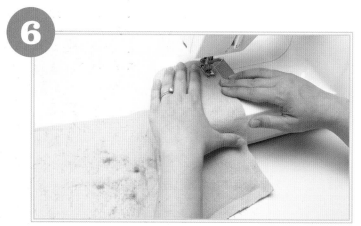

Assemble and sew pillow

With right sides together, stitch the cotton fabric to the embellished wool fabric using a ½" (1cm) seam allowance. Along the bottom of the pillow, leave an opening large enough for your hand. Diagonally snip the corners of the seam allowances to ensure that when you turn the pillow right-side out it will have nice pointed corners.

7

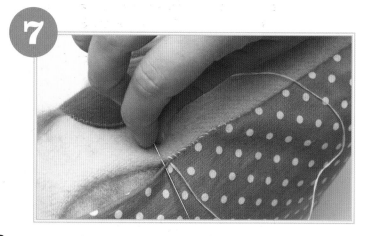

Turn, stuff and sew pillow

Turn the pillow right-side out. Stuff the pillow with polyester filling. With a sewing needle and thread, whipstitch the opening closed.

variation * Sachet

MATERIALS

* Wool roving—dark turquoise and olive green
* Wool fabric—¼ yard (23cm)
* Cotton fabric—¼ yard (23cm)
* Wool felt—light blue
* Polyester filling
* Lavender or other aromatic dried flowers or herbs
* Thread
* Felting needle
* Foam work surface
* Sewing needle
* Fabric scissors
* Tape measure

1

Cut base fabric and appliqués

Cut a 7½" x 7½" (19cm x 19cm) piece of wool fabric for the front of the sachet. Repeat with the cotton fabric for the backing. Needle felt wisps of dark turquoise and olive green wool roving for grass onto the wool fabric. Cut the tulip shapes (page 117) from the wool felt. Use a contrasting thread to zigzag stitch the tulip shapes onto the felted wool fabric.

2

Stuff sachet

With the right sides together, stitch the embellished wool fabric to the cotton fabric using a ½" (1cm) seam allowance. Leave an opening along the bottom of the sachet. Diagonally snip the corners of the seam allowances. Turn the sachet right-side out and stuff it with polyester filling and a bit of lavender. Close the opening with a whipstitch.

Forest Floor Pincushion

This fun little pincushion uses hand-spun wool yarn to mimic the texture of bark. A bonus of using a wool pincushion: The lanolin in the wool keeps your pins from rusting!

MATERIALS
* Wool roving—brown and tan
* Wool felt—green
* Wool stuffing
* Wool yarn—brown, hand-spun
* Felting needle
* Foam work surface
* Wood skewer
* Scissors

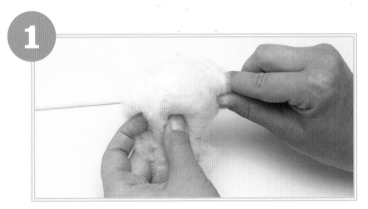

1

Create core for stump
Wind a large tuft of wool stuffing around a skewer. Pull the tuft off the skewer and needle felt it into a cylinder shape.

2

Wrap with wool roving
Cover the entire core with the brown wool roving and cover the top of the stump with the tan wool roving. Needle felt all of the wool roving onto the core.

3

Create branch with skewer
Wind a small tuft of brown wool roving around a skewer, pull the tuft off the skewer and needle felt that tuft to make a branch. Apply the tan wool roving to the top of the branch and needle felt the tan wool roving to attach it.

4

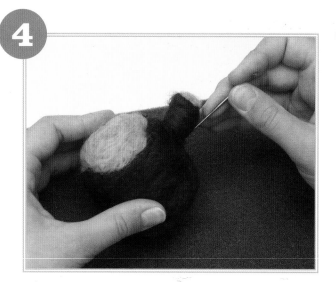

Attach branch

Hold the brown end of the branch against the side of the stump. Needle felt around the base of the branch and into the stump until the branch is securely attached. Give it a tug to make sure it's secure.

5

Create bark

Needle felt lengths of brown hand-spun yarn onto the stump. Curve the yarn and wind it into a spiral to mimic the look of bark.

6

Attach leaves

Cut 3 small leaf shapes from wool felt. Use a felting needle to attach the leaves to the stump near the branch.

FUN IDEAS

* Make seasonal pincushions! Add flowers for spring or fall-colored leaves for fall.

* Perch a little birdie on the stump, or make a wee gnome to accompany your pincushion!

Toadstools

MATERIALS

* Wool roving—red and white
* Felting needles
* Foam work surface
* Wood skewer

Create toadstool tops
Roll red wool roving into 3 small balls. Needle felt each ball of wool roving; flatten 1 side.

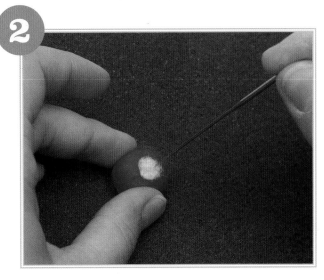

Add polka dots
Roll very small tufts of white wool roving to form loose ball shapes. Needle felt these to the top of each red mushroom cap to form polka dots.

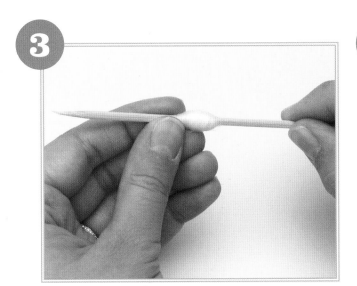

Make toadstool bases
Wind white wool roving into a tiny cylinder shape around a skewer. Remove the wool from the skewer. Use a felting needle to attach the stems to bottom of the toadstools. Repeat 2 times for a total of 3 stems.

Attach toadstools to stump
Use a felting needle to attach the toadstools to the top of the pincushion.

Birdie Album Cover

This photo album cover was inspired by colorful vintage crewel embroidery. By using bright colors and outlining the design in yarn, you can achieve this look without working even one stitch. Wool felt is used as the base fabric since it won't fray and is very forgiving to work with (no sewing required!).

This idea can be applied to any photo album, journal or scrapbook.

MATERIALS

* Wool roving—dark turquoise, olive green and orange
* Wool felt—light blue, large enough to cover the album
* Wool yarn—brown and hot pink
* Photo album
* Fabric glue
* Pinking shears
* Felting needle
* Foam work surface
* Air-soluble marking pen for fabric
* Fabric transfer paper
* Ruler

1

Measure felt

Open the photo album and lay it on the light blue felt. Measure around the photo album: flush with the top and bottom edges of the photo album, add 3" (8cm) on each side to create flaps that will attach to the inside of the front and back covers. Mark the measured rectangle with an air-soluble marking pen. Use pinking shears to cut a felt rectangle.

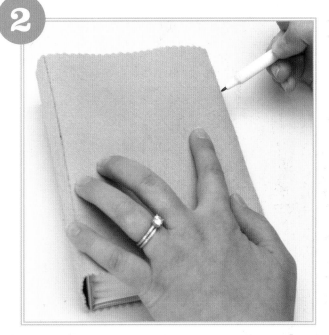

2

Mark fold lines on fabric

Wrap the rectangle around the closed photo album; fold the end flaps inside the front and back covers. To determine the boundaries of the design, use an air-soluble marking pen to mark the left and right edges of the front cover.

FUN IDEAS

* Flip through vintage embroidery books or clip-art books to find fun designs to transfer to your photo album cover and replicate the design in felt.

* Don't stop at the front cover; needle felt the spine and the back as well.

3

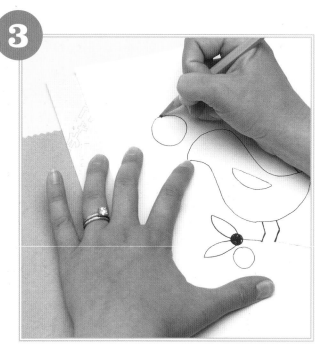

Trace design onto cover

Photocopy the design template (page 119). Depending on the size of your album, you may need to enlarge this template. Use transfer paper to transfer the design between the marked lines on the cut blue felt.

4

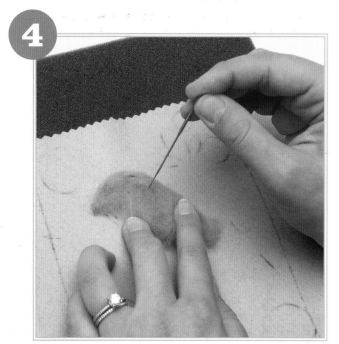

Needle felt wool roving to photo album cover

Lay the rectangle on a foam work surface. Starting with the wool roving for the bird's body, fill in the design. Needle felt the wool roving until it's smooth. Repeat for the other wool roving colors.

TIP

* Be sure to needle felt with the cover on the foam work surface, not directly on the photo album.

5

Outline with yarn

Lay the hot pink wool yarn around the bird, circles and leaves. Needle felt the yarn to attach it to the felt cover. Needle felt the brown yarn to the cover to create a branch.

6

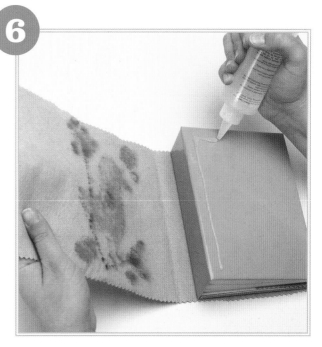

Glue cover to album

Use fabric glue to adhere the needle-felted cover to the photo album. Fold and secure the flaps inside the front and back covers.

Fabric Artwork

This project is sort of a "felt-by-number" piece, if you will. Pick a graphic fabric that you love, and fill in the design with wool roving! This is an easy way to create a textural, colorful masterpiece to hang in your home. No artistic skills are required! This is also a great way to use up scraps of wool roving you may have accumulated.

MATERIALS

* Wool roving—brown, dark turquoise, orange pink, white and yellow
* Wool yarn—brown, dark turquoise, orange, pink, white and yellow
* Cotton or linen fabric—11" × 14" (28cm x 36cm) (Fabric shown from Fabric Traditions)
* Frame with mat—11" × 14" (28cm x 36cm)
* Felting needle
* Foam work surface
* Tailor's pencil, chalk or air-soluble marking pen

1

2

3

Outline photo mat on fabric

Lay the frame's mat on the fabric, and frame the portion you want to needle felt. Mark the mat's inner border on the fabric with a tailor's pencil, chalk or an air-soluble pen.

Begin needle felting design

Lay the fabric on a foam work surface and begin needle felting the design with matching wool roving. It's best to use a single felting needle for this; you may be working in small areas and you can shape the wool roving or yarn as you needle felt it in place. If the design has thin lines, needle felt wool yarn onto these areas.

Check that wool roving is bonding

As the wool begins to felt onto the fabric, peel the fabric from the foam work surface—the wool roving will tend to stick to the foam—to assure that the wool roving is bonding with the fabric. If you can see that the wool roving has penetrated the fabric, then it's bonded.

4

Complete needle felting and frame

Use wool roving to fill in the background color, or you may want to leave this area blank, for a nice contrast. Place the mat on the felted fabric and secure it with tape or glue, if necessary. Place the matted fabric in a frame and hang the piece for everyone to enjoy. (You may leave out the frame's glass to allow people to experience the texture of the wool.)

FUN IDEAS

* Purchase fabric with the same pattern in various color schemes and make multiples to create a great set!

* Instead of framing your fabric artwork, staple it to a chunky little canvas!

* Stitch your felted art to a tote for a unique accessory, or whip up a pillow!

* Experiment with your own design on white cotton fabric. Either design directly on the fabric, or use transfer paper to transfer any drawings you have sketched on paper.

Art Deco Flowers Handbag

Mimicking the circular shape of the bag, these flowers were inspired by the blooms on a vintage candy tin. This bag is a unique addition to any ensemble!

MATERIALS

* Wool roving—dark turquoise, orange and red
* Wool felt—green and red, ½ yard (46cm) each
* Cotton fabric—orange, ¼ yard (23cm)
* Thread
* Sewing Machine
* Felting needle
* Foam work surface
* Fabric scissors
* Straight pins
* Tailor's pencil, chalk or air-soluble fabric marking pen
* Pencil or pen
* Iron
* Turning tool

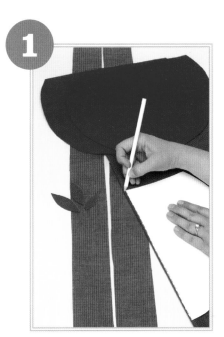

Trace and cut pattern pieces

If your green felt isn't folded, fold it in half lengthwise. Trace the template (page 120) onto the green felt with the dotted line on the fold. Cut 2. Then, cut 2 pieces of red felt for the lining, using the pattern. (Note: The lining is a bit shorter than the body of the bag.) Cut 2 pieces of orange cotton fabric [25" × 2½" (64cm x 6cm)] for the handles. Cut 3 leaves from the green wool felt.

Trace design

Transfer the flower design from the template (page 120) onto the green felt pieces from step 1.

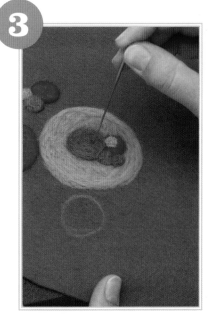

Needle felt design

Lay the green felt onto the foam work surface. Lay out the wool roving to fill in the design. Needle felt the wool roving in place.

4

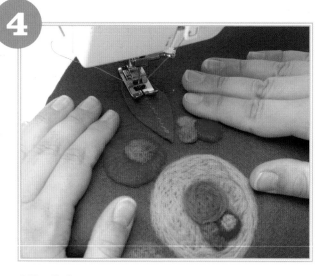

Attach leaves

Stitch the leaves onto the green felt pieces using a zigzag stitch running down the middle of each leaf.

5

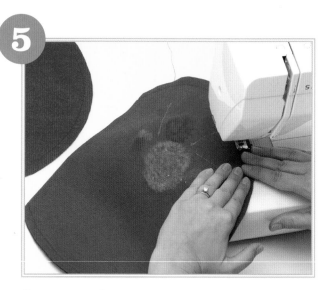

Sew bag and lining

Stitch the green felt pieces with the right sides together to form the body of the bag. Leave a ½" (1cm) seam allowance. Turn the bag right-side out. Stitch the red felt together for the lining, leaving a ½" (1cm) seam allowance. Be sure to leave an opening at the bottom of the lining for turning the lining right-side out later.

6

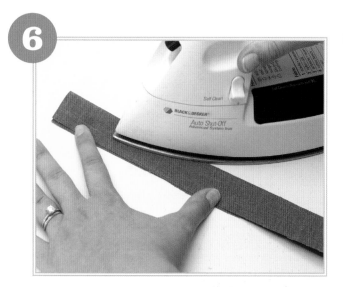

Press and sew handles

Fold the handle pieces in half lengthwise with the right sides together and press them with an iron. Stitch the right sides of a handle together with a ¼" (6mm) seam allowance. Repeat for the other handle.

7

Turn and press handles

Using a turning tool, turn the handles right-side out. Press each handle with an iron.

8

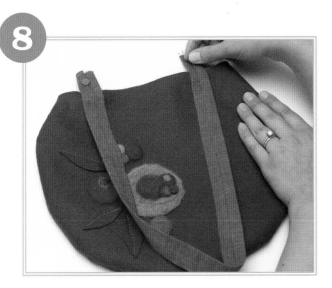

Pin handles to bag

Pin the right sides of the handles to the right side of the bag body along its top edge. Line up the raw edges of the handles with the top edge of the bag. (The handles will be upside down.)

9

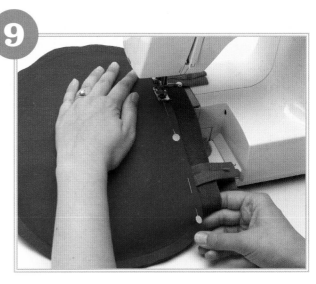

Sew lining to bag

Place the body of the bag inside the lining with the right sides together. Be sure to tuck in the handles. Stitch around the top edge of the bag.

10

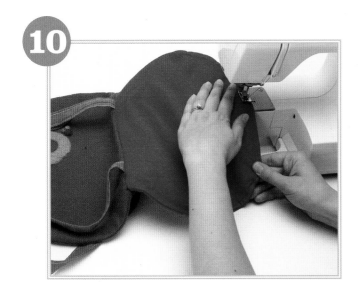

Turn, stitch and press bag

Pull the body of the bag and the handles through the opening in the bottom edge of the lining. Press with an iron. Stitch the opening in the lining closed with the sewing machine. Run the stitch along the bottom edge of the lining with no seam allowance. This not only closes the opening but also gives the bag a bit of structure. Push the lining down inside the body of the bag. Press the bag with an iron.

FUN IDEA

*Make a sweet little change purse to match your new handbag.

Woolly Wallet

This project is positively "no-sew"! That's why needle felting is so wonderful—you can create beautiful, artful objects and accessories with very little skill, tools or time. Create your own felt fabric from scratch and fold it into a snappy little wallet for stashing cash or makeup. You can make this wallet as small or as large as you'd like, based on how much wool and time you have!

MATERIALS

* Wool roving—light turquoise and orange
* Wool yarn—light turquoise
* Yarn needle
* Multineedle tool
* Felting needle
* Foam work surface
* Ruler

1

Lay out wool roving

Lay the tufts of light turquoise wool roving horizontally on a foam work surface to create a rectangle about 8" × 11" (20cm x 28cm), not including the wispy ends. Place an even layer of the light turquoise wool roving tufts vertically on top of the layer of horizontal tufts.

2

Needle felt wool roving

Needle felt the wool roving tufts together using a multineedle tool (to speed things up) until the fibers have bonded together.

3

Flip fabric and continue to needle felt

Peel the felted fabric off the foam and flip the fabric over. Fold over any wispy ends and needle felt them in place to create a clean edge. You should have a rectangle that measures approximately 7½" × 10½" (19cm x 27cm). Keep flipping and needle felting until the fibers are firmly bonded into a piece of felt fabric.

Add embellishments

Use orange wool roving to needle felt a circle onto the top third of the wallet. Needle felt another circle onto the bottom third of the light turquoise rectangle. Needle felt a long oval shape onto the middle third of the rectangle.

Attach yarn ties

Run a 15" (38cm) length of yarn down the rectangle to the left of the embellishments. Repeat on the right side of the embellishments. Keep 1 end of each length of yarn flush with an edge of the rectangle and let the long ends extend beyond the opposite edge. The third of the rectangle with the long yarn ends will be the top flap of your wallet. Needle felt each length of yarn in place.

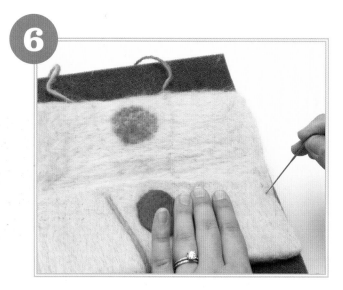

Needle felt sides to create seams

Flip over the rectangle, then fold up the bottom third onto the middle third of the rectangle. Needle felt along both sides to join these 2 parts and create a seam. Needle felt the seams until they are firmly joined.

Create ties

Thread light turquoise yarn onto a yarn needle and tie a knot in the other end of the yarn. Poke the threaded needle from inside the wallet through the bottom, on the fold, so that this yarn lines up with a yarn tie on the top flap. Repeat to create a yarn tie for the other yarn tie on the top flap.

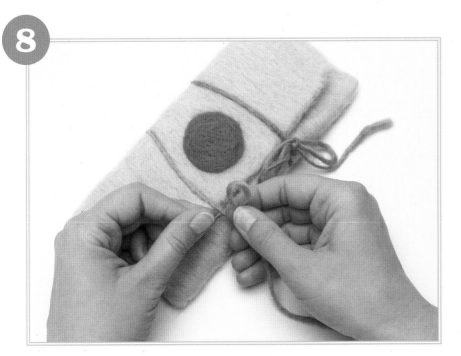

Close wallet

Fold down the upper flap and tie together each pair of yarn ties to hold the wallet closed.

FUN IDEAS

* Go wild with your design! Here it's simple, but you can mix up the colors and combine embellishment techniques to create a one-of-a-kind accessory.

* Add some glitz with sequins or beads. Isn't everything better with some sparkle?

* Make a mini size wallet for a change purse. Make a larger one for a clutch. Make multiples for gifts!

* Skip the ties and stitch on a snap or some Velcro to close the wallet.

Basket-Weave Bowl

Why not weave a basket from wool? Well, the basket is not completely woven, but it has the effect. This artful bowl is a great way to display your felt fruit (page 108).

MATERIALS

* Wool roving—hot pink, mint green and olive green
* Foam hat form—extra small
* Felting needle
* Multineedle tool (optional)

Wrap and needle felt wool roving
Wrap tufts of the olive green wool roving horizontally around the foam hat form and across the rounded top of the foam hat form. Needle felt all these tufts of wool roving to the foam hat form.

Apply second layer of wool roving
Place tufts of the olive green wool roving vertically on the sides of the foam hat form and over the first layer of wool roving. On the top of the foam hat form, lay tufts of olive green wool roving opposite the direction that you used in step 1. Needle felt these tufts of wool roving.

Create rim of bowl

Flip the foam hat form and wool roving so that the bare flat part is on the top. Wrap a horizontal layer of olive green wool roving along the top edge of the bowl; this forms the rim of the bowl. Needle felt this wool roving until the fibers have bonded.

Flip and needle felt bowl

Peel the bowl off the foam hat form, turn the bowl inside out, and place it back on the hat form. Needle felt all the wool roving. Continue turning and needle felting the bowl until you reach the desired consistency.

Create basket weave

Tear 12 sections of the olive green wool roving long enough to extend from the bowl's rim to the center of the bottom plus 1" (3cm). [The sections shown here are each approximately 7" (18cm).] Fold 1" (3cm) of a wool roving section under itself and needle felt this folded part to the bowl's rim; leave the rest of the wool roving section loose for weaving. Repeat with the remaining 11 wool roving sections so that they're evenly spaced around the bowl. Use a felting needle to tack the end of a rope of mint green wool roving that's long enough to circle the bowl and under an olive green wool roving section. Weave the mint green wool roving over and under the olive green sections around the bowl until it meets the attached end. Needle felt to secure this end.

6

Complete horizontal weave

With another rope of mint green wool roving, repeat the weaving portion of step 5 to form the second row; start an olive green section over from the start of the previous mint green row. Repeat until you have enough horizontal rows. Lightly needle felt all of the woven wool roving to secure the basket weave to the bowl.

7

Embellish rim of bowl

Needle felt a strip of hot pink wool roving to the rim of the bowl.

chapter 4

Dolls and Doodads

If you're fond of all things cute, then you'll love making these dolls, wee animals and other charming creations. From only a tuft of wool roving, you can create a woolen whimsy sure to brighten up anyone's day! You can now take my signature design to create your own *Cute and Cuddly Critters* (page 82). The *Birdie Mobile* (page 92) is a lovely addition to a new baby's nursery or any spot that requires a sweet touch! Give that little someone in your life a gift to treasure with *Miss Penelope Poppet* (page 110), a tried-and-true felt friend. Whether you intend to give your creations to little ones or to keep them for yourself, these projects are meant to bring a smile.

Cute and Cuddly Critters

While patterns (page 122) will help you shape these critters, needle felting will produce unique results depending on the wool you use, how firmly you needle felt, etc. There are no real rules, which is one thing I love about needle felting and that makes it a great medium for personalization and expression.

MATERIALS

* Wool roving—brown, tan and white
* Wool stuffing
* 4mm Black beads
* 28-gauge wire
* Small buttons (4)
* Monofilament (for cat and bunny whiskers)
* Upholstery thread
* Embroidery thread (optional)

* Felting needles
* Foam work surface
* Long sewing needle
* Doll-making needle
* Bamboo skewer
* Needle-nose pliers
* Round-nose pliers
* Superglue
* Cotton swabs (optional)
* Blush—powdered (optional)

Critter Body (bear shown)

1

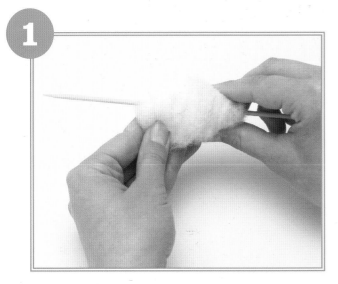

Create body core

Pull a tuft of wool stuffing about the size of a baseball, then wrap it tightly around a bamboo skewer to form a rounded sausage shape. Slide the wool stuffing off of the skewer, and place the wool stuffing on a foam work surface. Needle felt the wool stuffing, securing the wispy ends first, until the wool core is firm and about the size of a small egg.

2

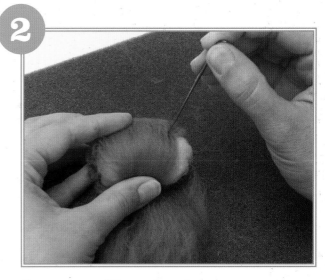

Cover core with wool roving

Pull a tuft of brown wool roving that's long enough to circle the core. Gently spread the tuft of wool roving to cover the core from end to end. Begin wrapping the wool roving around the core; needle felt the wool roving in place as you go. Be sure to cover the ends of the core. Continue needle felting until you have fully covered the core. Add more wool roving as needed to cover any bare spots. Keep needle felting until the wool roving is smooth.

3

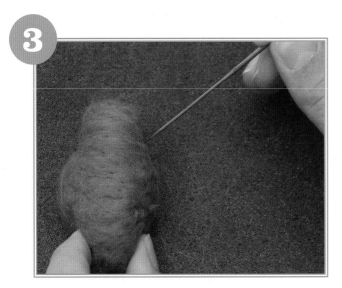

Make space for arms and legs

Needle felt indentations where you will attach the arms and legs.

4

Create limbs

Pull tufts of brown wool roving for the limbs. Make sure each pair of limbs is equally sized; make the legs a bit larger than the arms. Wrap a tuft of wool roving around a bamboo skewer into a small sausage shape, pull the tuft off the skewer and needle felt the tuft until the limb is firm. Repeat this to finish the other 3 limbs.

Bear Head

1

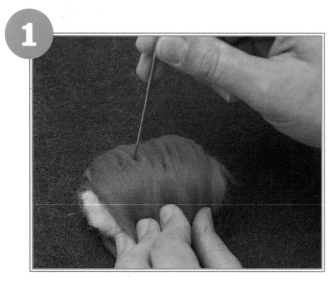

Form and cover core for the head

Pull a tuft of wool stuffing about the size of a grapefruit. Lightly needle felt the wool stuffing to create a core about the size of a jumbo egg. Cover the core with brown wool roving. Needle felt the brown wool roving.

2

Make ears

Wind 2 equal-sized tufts of brown wool roving into balls, each about the size of a quarter. Needle felt each ball of wool roving until it's firm; turn it as you go to ensure you achieve a round ball. Needle felt in the center of each ball to make an ear indentation.

3

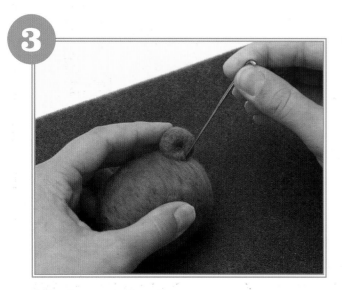

Attach ears to head

Position each ear as desired and needle felt around the ears to secure them to the head. Adjust the ear's shape as necessary by needle felting down through the top of the ear. Needle felt a small tuft of wool roving around the base of each ear to cover the seam between the ear and the head, if desired.

4

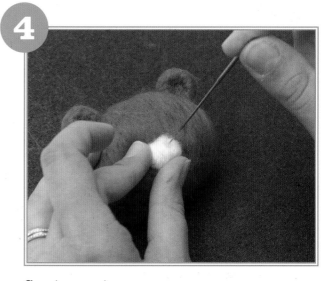

Create snout

Needle felt a small ball from white wool roving. Needle felt this ball to the middle of the face. Needle felt around and through the ball until the snout is securely attached to the face.

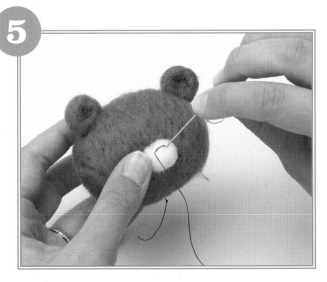

Embroider facial features

Thread upholstery thread or embroidery thread onto a sewing needle and tie a knot at the other end of the thread. Push the needle in through the bottom of the head and out through the face or snout, wherever you want to begin embroidering the nose or mouth. If your critter has a nose, start with that to help you center the mouth.

Embellish face

After you finish embroidering the facial features, push the needle back out through the bottom of the head and tie off the thread. Snip the thread close to the head. If you can still see a bit of thread, needle felt it down into the head to bury it. For rosy cheeks, apply blush with a cotton swab.

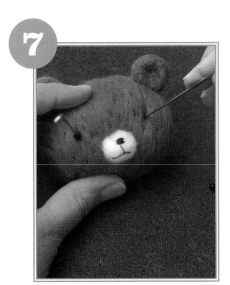

Place eyes

Position black beads on the face and use felting needles to hold them in place. Reposition each bead as necessary until you are happy with the placement. Needle felt a small indentation on the face for each eye.

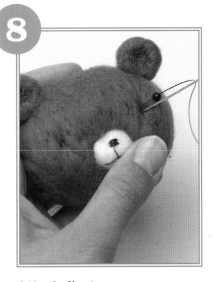

Attach first eye

Thread black upholstery thread into a needle that's long enough to span between the bear's eyes and thin enough to pass through each bead. Tie a knot in the other end of the thread. Push the needle in through the bottom of the head and pull the thread to secure the knot. Push the needle out through the first eye location, thread on the bead and push the needle in where you want the eye located.

Attach second eye

Push the needle out where you want to position the second eye, thread the bead onto the needle, and push the needle in at the eye location. Push the needle out by the first eye and repeat with each eye once more to secure them. Push the needle out through the bottom of the head; tie off the thread and embed the knot as you did in step 6.

Paws

These critters aren't recommended for small children. For safety, use black wool roving instead of beads for the eyes. Make sure the ears and tails are firmly attached. Also, needle felt or stitch the joint limbs instead of using buttons. Even with these adjustments, I wouldn't recommend these cute figures for children under the age of five. Use your best judgment!

SAFETY TIP

Add paw pads
Needle felt a small circle of tan wool roving to the tip of each limb.

Begin paws
Thread upholstery thread onto a sewing needle and tie a knot in the other end of the thread. Push the needle in through the top of the limb and out where you want the claw to begin.

Add claws
Stitch 3 vertical lines from the edge of the paw pad across the end of the limb for claws. After completing the third line, push the needle back out through the top of the limb. Tie a knot in the thread and pull the thread back through the limb to secure it, exiting at any point on the limb. Snip off the excess thread. Add claws to the remaining limbs.

Bunnies and Kittens

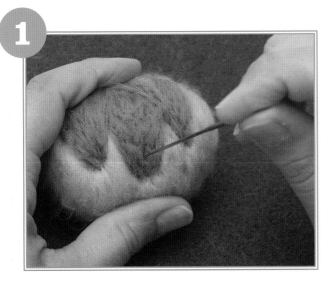

1

Create heads for other critters

Form and cover a core for the head (see step 1 on page 84). For the kitten, add stripes in a contrasting color of wool roving. Place 3 tufts of wool roving on the face, and needle felt the tufts in place. (Spots might be cute, too!)

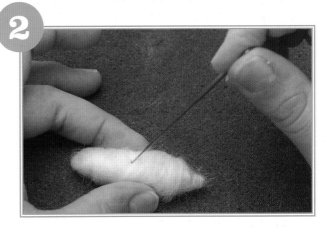

2

Create ears

Kitten: Needle felt a tuft of wool roving into a ball about the size of a quarter. Needle felt the top of the ball into a point by slightly flattening 1 top side and turning the ball over and flattening the other side. Use a contrasting color of wool roving to needle felt the inner part of the kitten's ear. Repeat to make the other ear.

Bunny: Wind a tuft of wool roving around a bamboo skewer to create a sausage shape. Pull the wool roving off the skewer. Needle felt the wool roving until it's firm; turn the wool roving around as you go and slightly flatten it to create a bunny's ear shape. Use a contrasting color of wool roving to needle felt the inner part of the bunny's ear. Repeat to make the other ear.

Attach the completed pair of ears to the head (see step 3 on page 84).

3

Add whiskers

Embroider the face and add the eyes (see steps 5–9 on page 85). Cut 3 equal lengths of monofilament. Thread a length of monofilament onto a needle, and push the needle through the face so that part of the monofilament extends from each cheek. Position the monofilament as desired. Add a tiny drop of superglue where the whisker meets the face, and pull the other end slightly so that the glued portion is inside the head to secure the whiskers. Repeat with the other 2 lengths of monofilament.

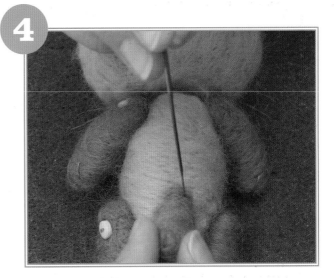

4

Add tails

Bunny: Roll white wool roving into a ball and needle felt it to the bunny as a tail.

Kitten: Wrap a small tuft of wool roving around a bamboo skewer into a long, skinny tail shape. Pull the tuft off the skewer and needle felt the wool roving. Needle felt each tail to its critter's body.

Attach Head

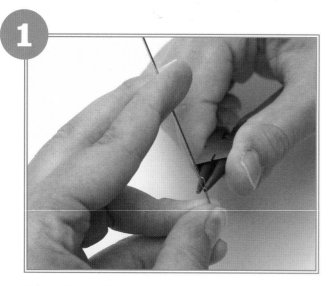

Thread needle

Thread wire onto a doll-making needle. Flatten the wire at the eye of the needle with needle-nose pliers to ensure that the wire will stay on the needle as you pull it through the body. Tie a knot at the other end of the wire.

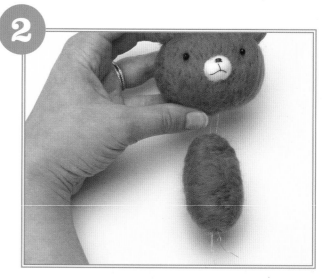

Attach head to body

Push the needle and wire in through the bottom of the critter's body, out through the top of the body, in through the bottom of the head and out through the top of the head. Pull the wire so that the knot meets the bottom of the body. Push the needle back in through the top of the head—this creates an indentation that you'll cover later—and out through the bottom of the body. (Avoid kinks in the wire as you pull it through, as they will get caught in the stuffing and wool roving.)

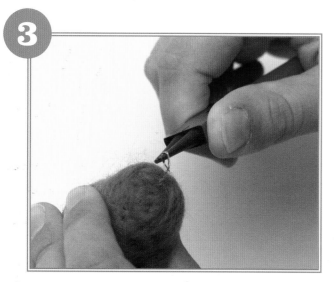

Secure wire and cover

Using round-nose pliers, twist the wire until it's secure and snip off excess but leave about 1/8" (3mm) of the wire. Twist the wire end up close to the body. Needle felt a small tuft of wool roving over the indentation at the top of the head.

FUN IDEAS

* Attach a bow to your critter with fabric glue.

* To make the kitten's hat as seen on page 82, follow the pattern (page 123). Roll the piece into a cone shape, and secure the cone's seam with fabric glue. Attach the hat to your critter's head by running a small bead of fabric glue along the inside rim of the hat and positioning the hat on the head. Embellish the hat as desired.

* To make skirt, follow the directions for the poppet's skirt (page 115). Scale the skirt to fit your critter.

Attach Limbs

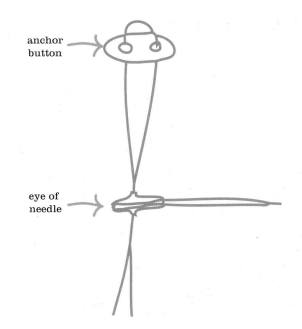

1

Thread needle

Cut approximately 24" (61cm) of upholstery thread. (I prefer to have more than I really need.) Thread the upholstery thread through both holes of a button; center the button in the middle of the piece of thread. Thread both ends of the upholstery thread onto a long sewing needle.

anchor button

eye of needle

2

Attach all limbs to body

Follow the path on the diagram at right to attach the limbs: Push the needle through the top of the outer side of the right arm and pull the button flush with the arm. Tie a knot inside the right arm. Push the needle in through the right shoulder and out through the left shoulder. Tie a knot against the left shoulder. Push the needle through the top of the left arm and through a button. Push the needle down through the other hole of that button, through the top of the left arm and out the right hip. Pull tight. Tie a knot against the right hip. Push the needle through the top of the right leg, through the first hole of another button, down through the other hole of that button, through the top of the right leg, in through the right hip, and out through the left hip. Tie a knot against the left hip. Push the needle through the top of the left leg, through 1 hole of the last button, down through the other hole of that button, through the top of the left leg, in through the left hip, and out through the bottom of the body. Tie a knot against the body, then push the needle in through the bottom of the body and out through the back ("END" on diagram). Pull the thread to pull the knot up inside the body; snip off the excess thread at the back. Use a felting needle to bury any remaining thread. Needle felt a tuft of wool roving over the thread and wire at the bottom of the body.

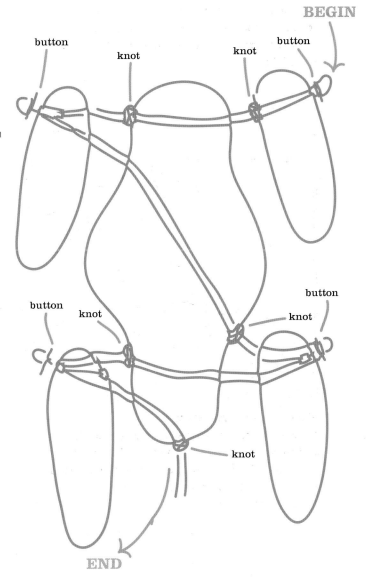

BEGIN

button   knot   knot   button

button   knot   knot   button

knot

END

ABC Beanbags

Kids love the squishy, weighty texture of these beanbags, and they enjoy tossing them about and creating little games.

This project is a great way to use up scraps of felted sweaters you may have left over from other projects—or to give life to a wool sweater you accidentally threw in the washer!

If you don't have any felted sweaters for this project, scour the racks for wool sweaters at a local thrift store; you might even find some outdated wool sweaters in your box of winter clothes. Throw the sweaters in your washer on hot (this time intentionally), and voilà, you'll have felted wool!

MATERIALS

* Wool roving—red
* Felted sweaters
* Letter stencils
* Dried beans or plastic pellets
* Felting needle
* Foam work surface
* Pinking shears
* Sewing machine
* Straight pins
* Funnel

Cut squares

Use pinking shears to cut felted sweater pieces into rectangles—mine are 5" × 7" (13cm × 18cm). You can adjust the size of your rectangles to fit your letter stencils. Cut 2 rectangles for every beanbag you want to make.

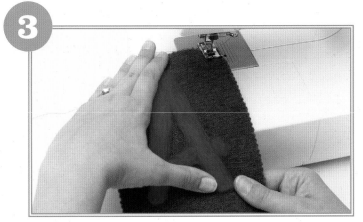

Needle felt wool roving in stencil

Lay a wool rectangle on a foam work surface. Place a letter stencil in the center of the rectangle and fill the stencil opening with tufts of red wool roving. Carefully needle felt the wool roving, staying within the stencil and shaping the wool roving with the needle as you go. Remove the stencil. Fill in any gaps in the letter with small tufts of wool roving and needle felt them in place. Repeat to make an embellished rectangle for every beanbag.

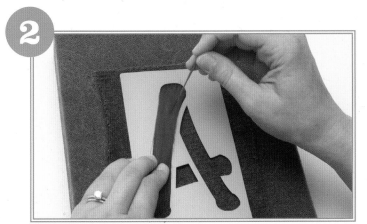

Sew front and back together

Use straight pins to pin a lettered rectangle to a blank rectangle and pin with wrong sides together. Zigzag stitch around all sides with a ½" (1cm) seam allowance; leave a small opening on any side. Be sure to backstitch at the beginning and end of each seam to secure the stitches. Repeat to assemble all of the beanbags.

Fill and finish

Place a funnel in the opening of a beanbag and fill it with about 1 cup of beans or pellets. Stitch the opening closed securely, so the beans or pellets won't spill out. Repeat to complete all of the beanbags.

Birdie Mobile

The soft textures and colors of this mobile make it perfect to hang in a baby's nursery or a child's room. Three woolly birds fly amid felt balls and flowers, creating an eye-catching display for your little one. Customize the colors to suit the décor!

MATERIALS

* Wool roving—hot pink, dark turquoise, light turquoise, lime green, olive green, orange and pink
* Wool stuffing
* Yarn
* Embroidery hoop—8" (20cm) diameter
* Fabric glue
* Felting needle
* Foam work surface
* Long, thick sewing needle
* Acrylic paint (optional)

Flowers and Felt Balls

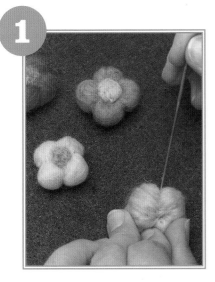

1

Create flower petals
Wind a tuft of pink wool roving into a ball and begin to needle felt it, but don't needle felt it to the point that it's firm. Needle felt the ball into quarters to create 4 petals.

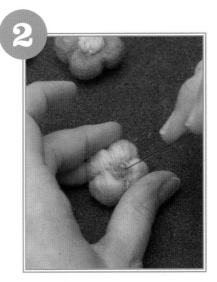

2

Add flower centers
Needle felt a small tuft of lime green wool roving where the petals meet at the center of the flower. Repeat steps 1 and 2 to make the desired number of flowers in multiple color combinations.

3

Create felt balls
Needle felt wool roving into multiple colors and sizes of felt balls.

Birds

1

Create bird core
Roll the wool stuffing in your hands to form 1 large ball and 1 ball that's about one-quarter of the size of the larger ball. Needle felt each ball so it retains its shape. Needle felt the smaller ball to the larger ball to form a core for the bird.

2

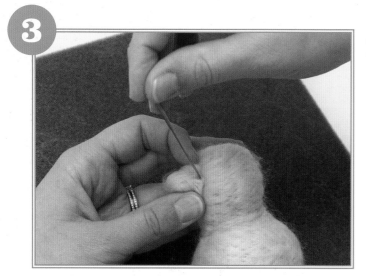

Cover core with wool roving
Wrap the light turquoise wool roving evenly around the core. Create the bird in the size and shape you like, or use my template (page 121) as a guide. Needle felt the wool roving to the core. Fill in the joint between the head and the body with the light turquoise wool roving. Needle felt the wool roving until the joint is smooth.

3

Add beak
Needle felt a small tuft of light turquoise wool roving to the head; shape the tuft into a beak.

4

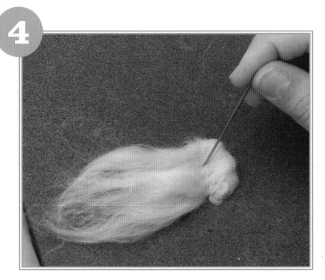

Make tail
Fold a tuft of light turquoise wool roving, and needle felt the folded end. Leave the wispy ends unfelted.

5

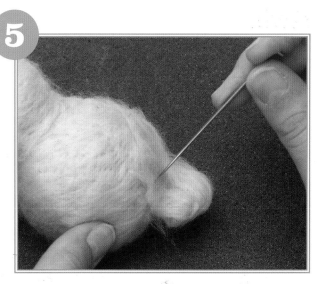

Attach tail
Use a felting needle to attach the wispy ends of the tail to the bird. Add more wool roving to build up the tail, and needle felt the tail to shape it.

6

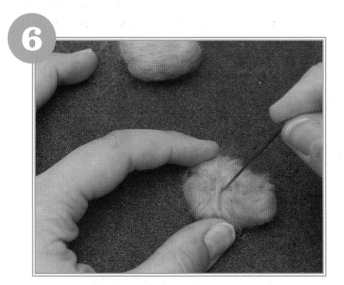

Create wings
Wind a tuft of lime green wool roving into a ball, and needle felt the ball to flatten it. Taper an end to shape the ball into a wing. Repeat to make the other wing. Needle felt the wings to attach them to the body. Repeat steps 1–6 to make 2 more birds.

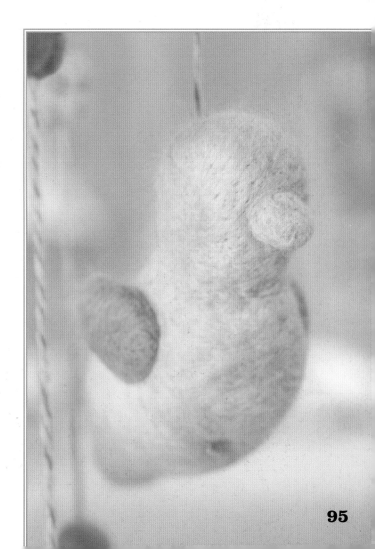

Mobile

1

Wrap or paint frame
Wrap yarn around the embroidery hoop; use fabric glue to secure the yarn to the hoop as you go. You can use acrylic paint to cover the embroidery hoop instead of wrapping it, if you prefer.

2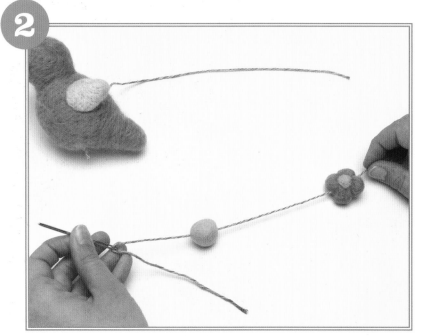

Thread mobile strings
Cut 3 equal lengths of yarn. Thread a length of yarn onto a long, thick sewing needle; push the needle into the bird's back and out through the bottom of the bird, then knot the yarn on the bottom. Repeat this for the remaining 2 birds.

Cut 3 more equal lengths of yarn that are slightly longer than the yarn for the birds. Using the same sewing needle, string the flowers and felt beads onto each length of yarn. Be sure to knot the bottom of each yarn length.

3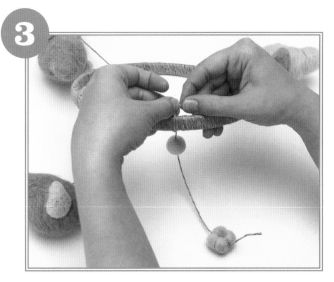

4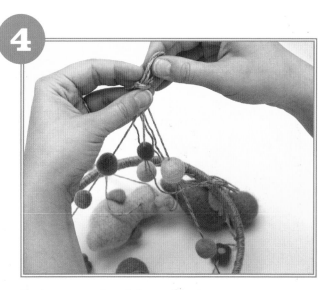

Attach strings to hoop

Tie all of the strings from step 2 to the embroidery hoop. Adjust the strings so they are evenly spaced on the hoop.

String top of mobile

Cut 3 more equal lengths of yarn and tie the end of each to the embroidery hoop. Use the sewing needle to string 2 felt balls onto each yarn length. Gather the 3 yarn lengths; pull 1 or more as needed to make sure the mobile hangs evenly. Leave at least 3"–4" (8cm–10cm) for the top loop. The size of the loop largely depends on how much excess you have and how large you want your loop to be. Tie a knot to join the tops of the 3 yarn lengths.

5

Thread yarn and finish

Thread the 3 yarn ends above the knot from the previous step onto the sewing needle, and push the needle through the middle of a felted flower. Pull the flower down close to the knot. Tie the loose yarn ends above the flower into a loop for hanging the mobile. Secure each knot on the mobile with a dab of fabric glue.

Catnip Mouse

Kitties love the texture of wool and, of course, the smell of catnip. Combine the two for a delectable treat for your feline. This project has been kitty tested and approved!

MATERIALS

* Wool roving—hot pink
* Small tufts of wool roving—black and white
* Small square of cotton fabric
* Wool yarn—brown
* Dried, loose catnip
* Fabric glue
* Felting needle
* Foam work surface
* Large yarn needle

1

Create catnip center

Place about 1 tablespoon of catnip in the center of a square [about 3" × 3" (8cm × 8cm)] of cotton fabric. Tie the square closed securely with a bit of yarn to form a little bundle.

2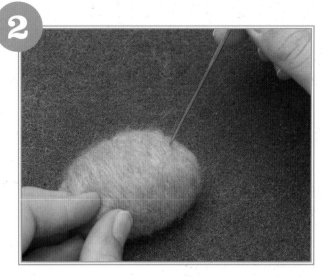

Cover center with wool roving

Wrap hot pink wool roving around the catnip bundle to form an egg shape. Needle felt the wool roving until it's firm; be sure to turn the piece as you go. It's OK to jab through to the catnip; this won't hurt the felting needle.

3

Add ears and facial features

Roll 2 small tufts of hot pink wool roving into tiny balls. Lightly needle felt each ball to bind the fibers. Needle felt the balls to the body to create ears. Needle felt small amounts of white and black wool roving onto the face of the body to create eyes and hot pink wool roving for the nose. To make whiskers, thread the brown wool yarn into a large needle and push the needle sideways through the nose. To secure the whiskers, put a drop of fabric glue where the whisker meets the face, then tug the other end of the yarn lightly to bury the glue behind the nose. Repeat to add another pair of whiskers.

4

Add tail

Thread the brown wool yarn onto a large needle, place a dab of glue on the end of the yarn to secure it and push the needle in through the nose and out through the rear of the mouse. Snip off the excess yarn at the nose, leaving only the yarn tail. Give this mouse to your kitty to enjoy!

FUN IDEAS

＊You can actually mix in some of your kitty's fur with the wool roving and needle felt the fur right into the mouse! This may sound weird, but kitties love it!

＊Try some different shapes, such as birds or fish.

Dog on Wheels

I have always been fascinated with vintage toys, especially stuffed animals. There is something so innocent and whimsical about a sweet old dog on wheels, but one can be expensive at an antique store!

This cute little dog is made for decoration, but you could add wheels that actually roll.

The finished dog stands about 5" (13cm) tall (not including the wheels) and 6" (15cm) long (not including the tail).

MATERIALS

* Corriedale or Romney wool roving—beige and brown
* Small bits of wool roving—black, pink and white
* Pipe cleaners (5)
* Wooden dowels—¼" (6mm) diameter to fit inside the hole of the wheels (2)
* Wooden wheels—1½" (4cm) diameter (4)
* Strong fabric glue
* Ribbon
* Red craft paint
* Felting needle
* Foam work surface
* Paintbrush
* Wooden skewer
* Glue—wood or all-purpose craft

Create skeleton

To create an armature, twist 2 pipe cleaners together. Twist 2 more pipe cleaners together. Then twist the 2 sets together to form an **X**. Bend down the end quarters to create 4 legs. Fold a pipe cleaner in half and twist the halves together to create the head. Join the head to 1 end of the legs and body between the front legs. Bend the head piece to create the neck and head.

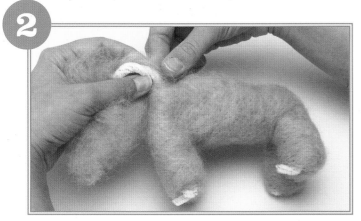

Wrap wool roving around armature

Begin wrapping beige wool roving around the body armature. Gently needle felt to secure the wool roving; carefully avoid the pipe cleaners. Layer on more wool roving and needle felt it until the body is about 2" (5cm) around. Wrap wool roving around the legs and needle felt it in place. Wrap wool roving around the area where the legs meet the body and needle felt the wool roving in place. Keep layering and needle felting to achieve a nice dog body. Wrap some wool roving around the neck area and needle felt it in place. Add wool roving to the head and snout area and needle felt it in place, building up and layering as necessary.

TIP

This project uses pipe cleaners to create an armature for the dog, which gives him a bit of structure and stability. Corriedale or Romney wool roving is best to use, as it is very crimpy; it grabs onto the pipe cleaners nicely, and it felts quite easily and seamlessly. These types of wool roving give a bit of a fuzzier look, but since this is a pooch, that's OK!

3

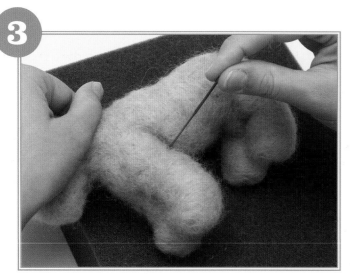

Needle felt to shape

Needle felt to finesse the shape by making a narrower hip region and adding creases to the area where the hind legs meet the body. Since pipe cleaners are the armature, you can bend the legs a bit and do some concentrated needle felting in the crook of the leg if necessary to create a crisper bend. Flatten the bottoms of the feet with a felting needle.

4

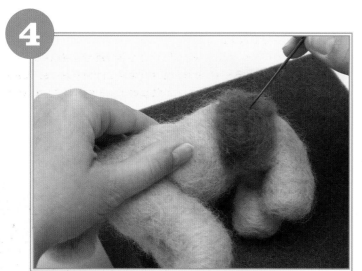

Give dog spots

Layer brown wool roving in random places to create spots. Needle felt these spots to blend them into the body.

5

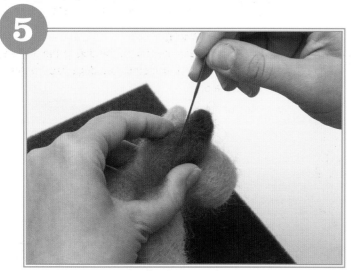

Add ears and tail

Needle felt a side of a small tuft of brown wool roving; leave the wispy ends unfelted. Concentrate the needle felting in 1 spot to create a bend in the ear. Needle felt to attach the wispy ends of the ear to the head. Repeat to make the other ear. For the tail, wrap a tuft of beige wool roving around a wooden skewer and form the wool roving into a little sausage shape. Pull the wool roving off the skewer and needle felt it until it's firm. Leave 1 end a bit loose; needle felt this end to the body with the felting needle.

6

Add lips and nose

For the muzzle, needle felt an indentation down the middle of the snout and curve it up on both sides. Needle felt a tiny bit of black wool roving inside the indentation to create a mouth. Needle felt a small black ball of wool roving onto the snout for a nose and a small bit of pink wool roving under the mouth for the tongue. For eyes, needle felt 2 tiny tufts of white wool roving onto the face and add a bit of black wool roving to each eye for the pupil. Tie a length of ribbon in a bow around the neck.

7

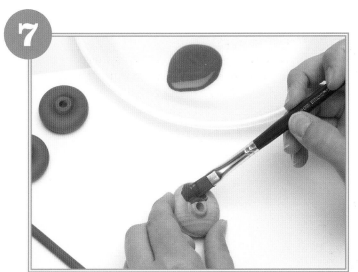

Make wheels

Paint the dowels and wooden wheels red and allow them to dry. Insert dowels inside the holes on the wheels. Use a bit of wood or all-purpose craft glue if necessary to secure.

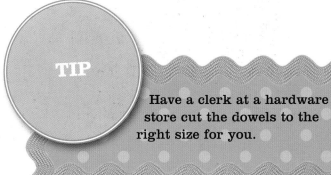

TIP

Have a clerk at a hardware store cut the dowels to the right size for you.

8

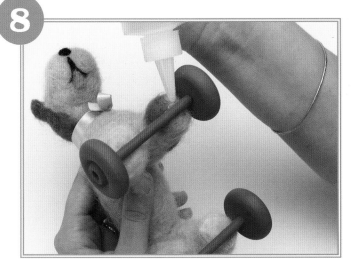

Attach wheels to dog

Use fabric glue to attach the feet of the dog to the dowels; allow the glue to dry. You can stitch the dog's feet to the dowels if you prefer.

SAFETY TIP

Don't forget: Tiny wheels are a choking hazard for little ones.

Cozy Cottage

I love all things miniature, and there is something magical and charming about tiny houses. Inspired by Art Deco images of cottages, I had to create one out of wool! This house is made with a small square of foam for a base and a small triangle of foam for the roof. This helps you to achieve a uniform shape and is handy when making multiple houses for a village.

It is hard not to get carried away when creating these houses. There are endless possibilities for designing the gardens and the houses themselves. You are limited only by your imagination!

MATERIALS

* Wool roving—dark turquoise, hot pink, light turquoise, lime green, olive green, orange, white and yellow
* Small piece of wool felt
* Upholstery foam— 1½" (4cm) thick
* Fabric glue
* Fabric scissors
* Round cookie cutter—4½" (11cm) diameter
* Felting needle
* Foam work surface
* Wooden skewer
* Pinking shears

House

1

Cut foam base pieces
Use fabric scissors to cut 2 cubes of 1½" (4cm) upholstery foam. Shape the cube into a triangle by cutting diagonally from 2 adjacent corners into the center of the square.

2

Cover with wool roving
Cover the square with light turquoise wool roving and needle felt it in place. Continue needle felting until the house is evenly covered and the wool roving is smoothly bonded. Repeat this process with the orange wool roving to cover the roof.

3
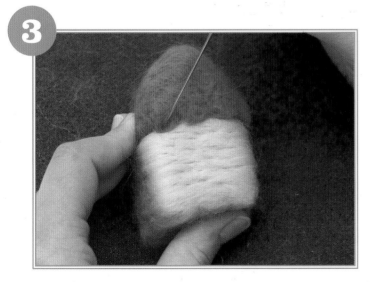

Attach roof
Use a bit of fabric glue to adhere the roof to the top of the house. After the glue dries, add some small tufts of the orange wool roving to conceal the joint between the roof and the house; needle felt this added wool roving to form a scalloped edge.

4

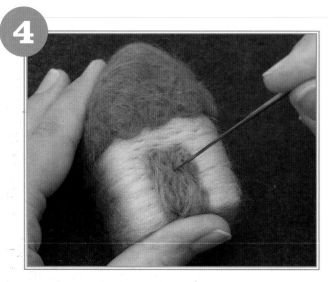

Add door
Needle felt dark turquoise wool roving into a rectangle for the door. Needle felt a dot of orange wool roving onto the rectangle for the doorknob.

5

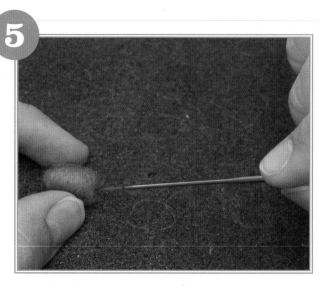

Construct chimney
Wrap a tuft of dark turquoise wool roving around a wooden skewer and form the wool roving into a small sausage shape. Pull the wool roving off the skewer. Needle felt this piece; flatten and square off an end— this end is the top of the chimney. Needle felt the rounded end of the chimney to attach it to the roof.

6

Make smoke
Roll a small tuft of white wool roving between your fingers to create a ball and needle felt it. Focus your needle felting to create an indentation to give a cloudy, puffy look to the smoke. Because this piece is so small, use fabric glue to attach it to the chimney.

FUN IDEAS

* Create an entire village. One for the holidays could be quite festive!

* Rather than gluing houses to the base, attach a bit of the hooked portion of Velcro to the bottom of each house to create an interchangeable play set for a child.

Lawn

1

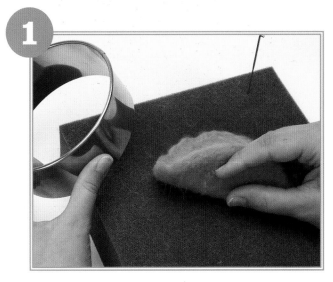

Create felt fabric lawn

Place a round cookie cutter on a foam work surface and fill the cookie cutter with 2 layers of lime green wool roving. Needle felt the wool roving. Peel the wool roving off the foam work surface, flip the wool roving over and needle felt the other side. Keep flipping and needle felting until the wool circle is firmly felted. Use a bit of fabric glue to attach the house to this circular lawn.

2

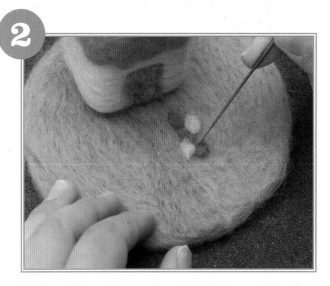

Make sidewalk

Needle felt hot pink wool roving to the lawn to form a pathway leading from the edge of the lawn to the house. Around the path, needle felt small dots of hot pink, orange and yellow wool roving to represent flowers.

3

Create trees and shrubs

For a tree, wrap a tuft of olive green wool roving around a wooden skewer. Remove the wool roving from the skewer, and needle felt it until firm; taper an end. Repeat this process on a smaller scale to make a shrub. Glue the tree and the shrub in place on the lawn.

4

Finish base

Using a round cookie cutter as a template, use pinking shears to cut a piece of wool felt. Use fabric glue to attach the felt to the underside of the lawn.

Fun Fruit

This fruit is much nicer than plastic fruit! Everlasting and textural, it adds a whimsical touch when displayed on a table or in a shadow box on the wall. These pieces of fruit could also be toys for the kiddies—just make sure the stem and leaves are securely attached!

You can make the fruit colors realistic or wild—add polka dots or stripes if you want wacky fruit!

MATERIALS

* Wool roving—brown, light turquoise, lime green and orange
* Wool stuffing
* Polka-dot cotton fabrics
* Fabric glue
* Felting needle
* Foam work surface
* Wooden skewer
* Pinking shears
* 28-gauge wire (optional)

1

Form core

Roll a handful of wool stuffing into a ball and needle felt it until it's moderately firm. It should be about three-quarters of the size you want your finished fruit to be. [The fruits shown at left are about 3½"–4½" (9cm–11cm) tall.] For a pear, add a smaller ball on top of the larger ball.

2

Cover core with wool roving

Wrap light turquoise wool roving around the core, and needle felt the wool roving in place until it's smooth, secure and nicely felted. Use lime green wool roving to make an apple and orange wool roving to make a peach.

3

Add indentations

Concentrate your needle felting in 1 spot on the bottom of the fruit. Repeat this on the top of the fruit; increasing the indentation's depth for an apple.

4

Create stem

Wrap a small tuft of brown wool roving around a wooden skewer and form the wool roving into a small sausage shape. Pull the wool roving off the skewer and needle felt the wool roving until it's firm. Needle felt the stem into the indentation on the top of the fruit. (Stitch the stem on if children will play with the fruit.)

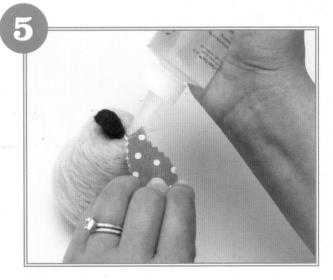

5

Add leaves

Use pinking shears to cut a leaf shape out of a piece of polka-dot fabric folded in half. To make a shape-able leaf, sandwich wire and fabric glue between the 2 leaves. Use fabric glue to attach the leaf to the fruit near the stem.

Miss Penelope Poppet

This doll was inspired by vintage German and Polish dolls. She is perfect for a child to play with—there are no bits that can come off and pose a choking hazard.

MATERIALS

* Wool roving—blue, brown, flesh, hot pink, light turquoise, olive green, orange and white
* Wool stuffing
* Wool felt—orange
* Fabric for skirt
* Cosmetic blush
* Yarn or ribbon
* Felting needle
* Foam work surface
* Wooden skewers
* Cotton swabs
* Iron
* Yarn needle
* Sewing machine
* Fabric scissors
* Multineedle tool (optional)

1

Create core
Wrap wool stuffing around a wooden skewer and form a long sausage shape 8" (20cm) long and 3" (8cm) in diameter.

2

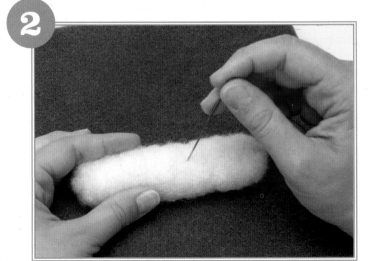

Form head
Shape the head by needle felting an indentation around the top quarter of the core to create the neck.

3

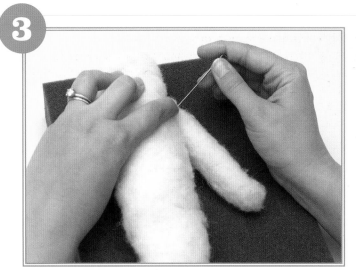

Add arms and legs

Wrap wool stuffing around a wooden skewer and form a sausage shape to serve as a limb. Pull the wool stuffing off the skewer and needle felt it to secure the fibers. Repeat this process to make 3 more limbs. Needle felt to attach each limb to the body.

4

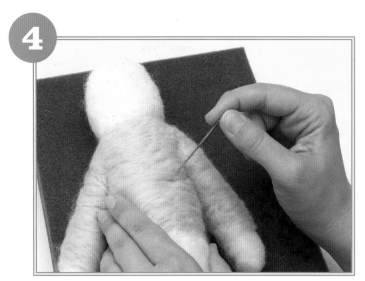

Needle felt shirt

Needle felt a layer of light turquoise wool roving from the neck to the waist and halfway down the arms to create a shirt.

5

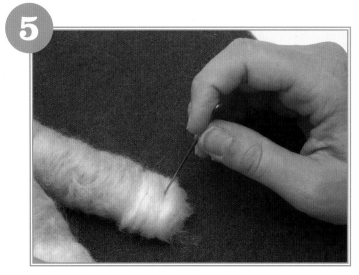

Add skin

Needle felt flesh-colored wool roving onto the head and the exposed arm areas.

6

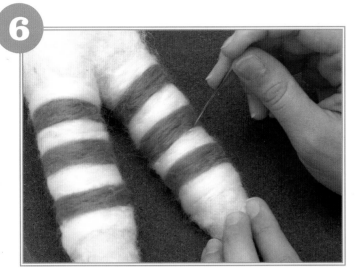

Create stockings

Needle felt alternating stripes of white and olive green wool roving up each leg. Leave the bottom of each leg uncovered.

7

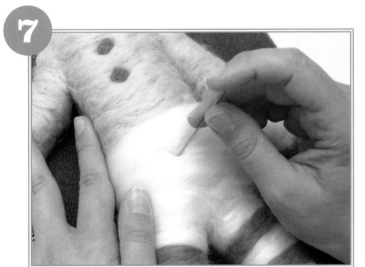

Add bloomers and buttons

Wrap white wool roving around the body from the stockings up to the shirt. Needle felt the white wool roving in place. Use olive green wool roving to needle felt 3 dots on the shirt to depict buttons.

8

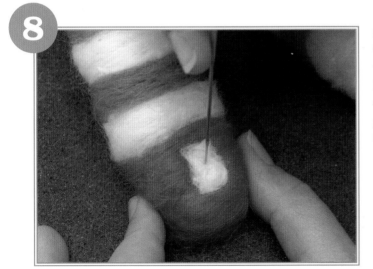

Create shoes

Wrap orange wool roving around each foot. Needle felt the wool roving to secure it. To make the shoes Mary Janes, needle felt a U-shaped bit of white wool roving to each shoe to mimic the stocking peeking through. Needle felt a bit of brown wool roving onto each shoe for a buckle.

Hair and Face

1

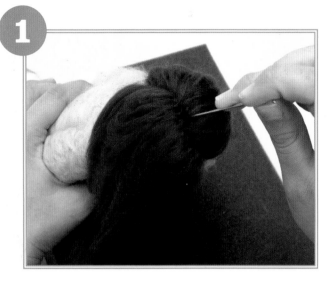

Attach and part hair

Pull 2 equal-sized tufts of brown wool roving. Needle felt the 2 tufts together on the top of the head to form the part in the hair. Lightly needle felt down both sides and the back of the hair to adhere it to the scalp. Tie each side with yarn or ribbon near the scalp if you want loose pigtails; otherwise, braid the wool roving on each side and tie yarn or ribbon at the end of each braid.

2

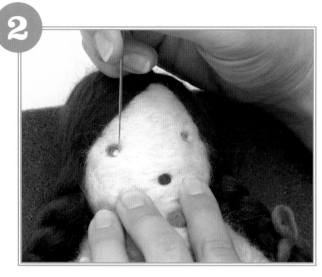

Add facial features

For the eyes, roll 2 tiny tufts of blue wool roving between your fingers to make 2 small balls. Needle felt the eyes to the face. Needle felt a bit of white wool roving to form the catchlight. For the mouth, needle felt a tiny tuft of hot pink wool roving in place. Use powdered cosmetic blush and a cotton swab to add rosy cheeks.

3

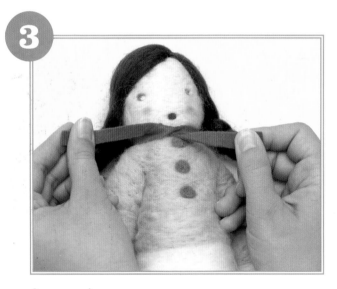

Accessorize

Tie a ribbon or a bit of wool felt around the neck to create a scarf and further define the neck.

Skirt

1

Cut fabric
Cut 2 pieces of fabric, each measuring 12" × 5" (30cm x 13cm).

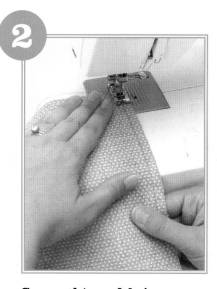

2

Sew and turn fabric
Stitch the 2 rectangles with right sides together with a ¼" (6mm) seam allowance; leave an end open. Turn the piece right-side out.

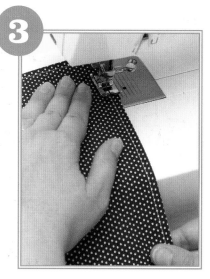

3

Finish edges of skirt
On the open end, tuck the fabric under ¼" (6mm) and press. Stitch around all 4 sides with a ⅛" (3mm) seam allowance.

4

Add tie to waist
Thread a length of yarn or thin ribbon into a yarn needle. Push the needle through 1 long side in the channel between the stitching and the outside edge. Hold the end of the ribbon or yarn so you don't pull it into the skirt waist.

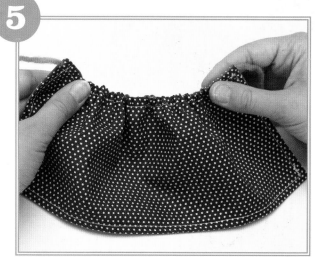

5

Gather waist
Push the skirt waist inward along the yarn or ribbon to gather it. Tie the skirt around the doll's waist and adjust the fabric for full coverage.

Flower Pin
(page 24)

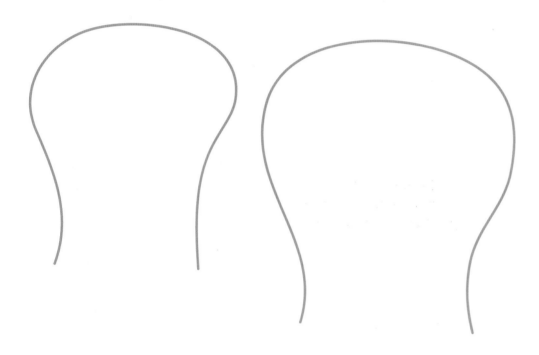

FLOWER PETALS
Use a photocopier to reproduce pattern at 100%.

Folk Belt

(page 34)

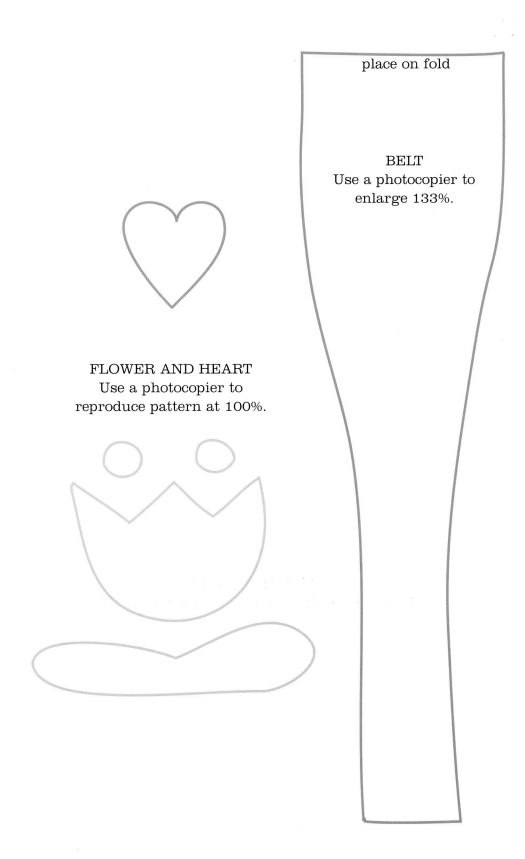

place on fold

BELT
Use a photocopier to
enlarge 133%.

FLOWER AND HEART
Use a photocopier to
reproduce pattern at 100%.

Wispy Pillow
(page 54)

BUTTERFLY BODY
Use a photocopier to
reproduce pattern at 100%.

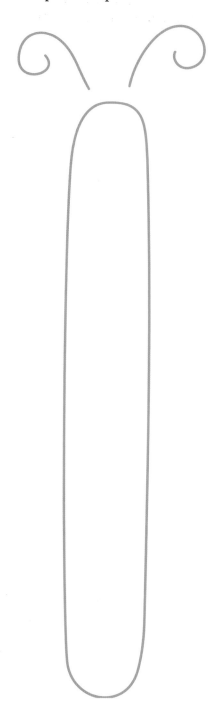

Birdie Album Cover

(page 62)

COVER DESIGN
Use a photocopier to
reproduce pattern at 100%.

Art Deco Flowers Handbag

(page 68)

PATTERN AND FLOWER DESIGN
Use a photocopier to
reproduce pattern at 100%.

top line for lining

place on fold

Birdie Mobile
(page 92)

BIRD
Use a photocopier to
reproduce pattern at 100%.

Cute and Cuddly Critters

(page 82)

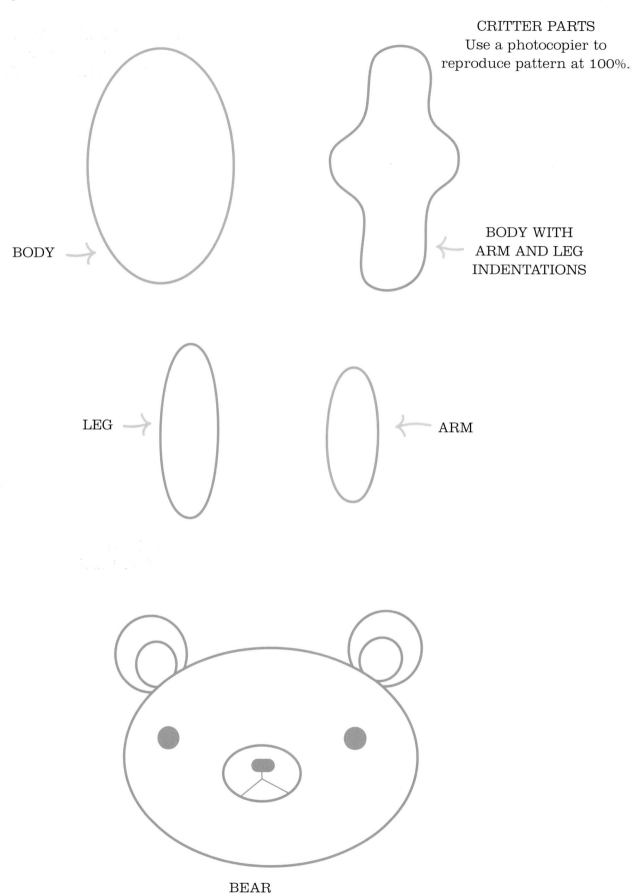

CRITTER PARTS
Use a photocopier to reproduce pattern at 100%.

BODY →

← BODY WITH ARM AND LEG INDENTATIONS

LEG →

← ARM

BEAR

Cute and Cuddly Critters, continued
(page 82)

CRITTER PARTS AND HAT
Use a photocopier to
reproduce pattern at 100%.

KITTEN

PARTY HAT
FOR KITTEN

BUNNY

Resources

 ## Wool Roving
www.marrhaven.com
www.theflyingewe.com
www.halcyonyarn.com
www.ornamentea.com

 ## Yarn
www.purlsoho.com

 ## Needle-Felting Tools
www.thefeltedewe.com
www.marrhaven.com
www.hookedonfelt.com

 ## Foam Forms
www.hookedonfelt.com

 ## Fabric
www.magiccabin.com
   (wool felt and wool stuffing)
www.achildsdream.com
   (wool felt and other supplies)
www.nationalnonwovens.com
   (wool felt)
www.oxfordmillendstore.com
   (wool fabric)
www.purlsoho.com
   (cotton fabrics)
www.fabrictraditions.com
   (cotton fabric)

Index

A

ABC Beanbags, 90-91
  materials, 90
  stencils, 91

accessory projects, women's, 34-37, 44-45, 47, 68. *See also* Art Deco Flowers Handbag; Folk Belt; Free-Form Rose Scarf; Wool and Tulle Winter Hat; Woolly Wallet

appliqués, 16, 35, 57. *See also* Folk Belt; Sachet

armatures, 21, 101. *See also* Dog on Wheels

Art Deco Flowers Handbag, 47, 68-71
  materials, 69
  transfer design, 69

B

balls, wool roving, 18, 25, 31, 32, 39, 61, 93, 09. *See also* Birdie Mobile; Flower Pin; Fun Fruit; Gumdrop Ring; Strawberry Necklace; Toadstools

Basket-Weave Bowl, 76-79
  embellishments, 79
  materials, 77

beads, wool roving, 18, 39. *See also* Strawberry Necklace

belt. *See* Folk Belt

Birdie Album Cover, 62-65
  fun ideas, 63
  materials, 63
  template, 119
  transfer design, 64

Birdie Mobile, 81, 92-97
  ball creation, 93
  core creation, 94
  materials, 93
  template, 121

bracelet. *See* Woolly Bangle Bracelet

C

Catnip Mouse, 98-99
  fun ideas, 99
  materials, 98

Circle Trivet, 53
  materials, 53

coasters. *See* Heart Coasters

cookie cutters, 9, 15, 48-49, 52, 53, 107. *See also* Circle Trivet; Cozy Cottage; Crazy for Circles Rug; Heart Coasters

cores, creating, 18, 59, 83, 84, 87, 94, 109, 111. *See also* Birdie Mobile; Cute and Cuddly Critters; Forest Floor Pin Cushion; Fun Fruit; Miss Penelope Poppet

Corriedale wool batting, 51

Corriedale wool roving, 8, 101

Cozy Cottage, 20, 104-107
  cookie cutter, 107
  foam forms, 104-105
  fun ideas, 106
  materials, 104
  skewers, 106-107

Crazy for Circles Rug, 50-53
  cookie cutter, 52
  embellishments, 52
  fun ideas, 53
  materials, 51
  variation, 53

Cute and Cuddly Critters, 81, 82-89
  core creation, 83, 84, 87
  embellishment, 85
  embroidery, 85
  fun ideas, 88
  materials, 82
  safety tip, 86
  skewers, 83
  template, 122-123

D

design-transfer devices, 9. *See also* transferring designs

Dog on Wheels, 100-103
  armature creation, 101
  dowels and wheels, 103
  materials, 101
  safety tip, 103
  skewer, 102

doll and toy projects, 81-91, 100-103, 110-115. *See also* ABC Beanbags; Birdie Mobile; Cute and Cuddly Critters; Dog on Wheels; Miss Penelope Poppet

E

embellishments, 9, 12, 37, 52, 55, 74, 75, 79, 84. *See also* Basket-Weave Bowl; Crazy for Circles Rug; Cute and Cuddly Creatures; Folk Belt; Strawberry Necklace; Wispy Pillow; Woolly Wallet; yarn
  beads, 9, 33, 40, 75

buttons, 9
sequins, 9, 75
trim, 9, 35

F

Fabric Artwork, 47, 66-67
  fun ideas, 67
  materials, 66

fabric resources, 124

felt fabric, making, 17

felting needles, 10

Flower Pin, 23, 24-25
  ball creation, 25
  fun ideas, 25
  jewelry findings, 25
  materials, 24
  template, 116

foam forms, 11, 104-105. *See also*
Basket-Weave Bowl; Cozy Cottage
  needle felting onto, 20
  online resources, 124

foam work surfaces, 11

Folk Belt, 34-35
  appliqués, 35
  embellishments, 35
  fun ideas, 35
  materials, 34
  template, 35, 117

Forest Floor Pincushion, 58-60
  core creation, 59
  fun ideas, 60
  materials, 59

foundation fabrics, 9

Free-Form Rose Scarf, 23, 44-45
  embellishment, 44
  fringe, 45
  materials, 44

Fun Fruit, 108-109
  ball creation, 109
  core creation, 109
  materials, 108
  skewers, 109
  wool stuffing, 109

G

Gumdrop Ring, 23, 30-33
  ball creation, 31, 32
  beads, 33
  embellishments, 33
  fun ideas, 31, 33
  jewelry findings, 33

materials, 31

H

handmade felt fabric, 12

hat. *See* Wool and Tulle Winter Hat

Heart Coasters, 47, 48-49
  cookie cutters, 48-49
  materials, 48

home accessories and décor projects, 47-57, 66-67, 76-79, 104-109.
See also Basket-Weave Bowl; Circle
Trivet; Cozy Cottage; Crazy for Circles
Rug; Fabric Artwork; Fun Fruit; Heart
Coasters; Sachet; Wispy Pillow

I

Internet resources, 124

J

jewelry findings, 11, 25, 33, 40-41.
See also Flower Pin; Gumdrop Ring;
Strawberry Necklace

jewelry projects, 23-33, 38-41. *See
also* Flower Pin; Gumdrop Ring;
Strawberry Necklace; Woolly Bangle
Bracelet

M

Materials, needle felting, 8-11

Merino wool, 8. *See also* Birdie
Album Cover; Catnip Mouse; Cozy
Cottage; Forest Floor Pincushion;
Toadstools

miscellaneous projects, 58-65, 98-99,
104-107

Miss Penelope Poppet, 81, 110-115
  core creation, 111
    fun ideas, 114
    materials, 111
    skewer, 111-112

multineedle tools, 10, 49, 51-52, 53,
73, 77-78. *See also* Basket-Weave
Bowl; Circle Trivet; Crazy for Circles
Rug; Heart Coasters; Woolly Wallet

N

Necklace. *See* Strawberry Necklace

needle felting, 7
  basic steps, 12-13
  free-form, 14
  safety, 13, 86, 103

needle felting tool resources, 124

needles. *See* felting needles; multineedle tools

P

patterns, transferring, 15. *See also*
transferring designs; templates

pillow. *See* Wispy Pillow

pin (jewelry). *See* Flower Pin

purse. *See* Art Deco Flowers
Handbag

R

resources, online, 124

ring. *See* Gumdrop Ring

Romney wool roving, 8, 101

rug. *See* Crazy for Circles Rug

S

Sachet, 57
  appliqués, 57
  materials, 57

safety tips, 13, 86, 103

scarf. *See* Free-Form Rose Scarf

sculptural pieces, 12, 58-61, 82-89,
98-99, 100-109. *See also* Catnip
Mouse; Cozy Cottage; Cute and
Cuddly Critters; Dog on Wheels;
Forest Floor Pincushion; Fun Fruit;
Toadstools

sewing machine. *See* ABC Bean-
bags; Art Deco Flowers Handbag;
Wispy Pillow; Miss Penelope Poppet;
Woolly Bangle Bracelet

skewers, shaping with, 19, 59, 60,
83, 102, 106-107, 109, 111-112. *See
also* Cozy Cottage; Cute and Cuddly
Critters; Dog on Wheels; Forest Floor

Pincushion; Fun Fruit; Miss Penelope Poppet; Toadstools

stencils, 15, 91. *See also* ABC Beanbags

Strawberry Necklace, 38-41
  ball creation, 39
  bead creation, 39
  fun ideas, 41
  jewelry findings, 40-41
  materials, 39
  seed beads, 40

T

templates, 116-123. *See also* Art Deco Flowers Handbag; Birdie Album Cover; Birdie Mobile; Cute and Cuddly Critters; Flower Pin; Folk Belt; Wispy Pillow
  using, 14

tips and suggestions, needle felting for foam forms, 20

Toadstools, 61
  materials, 61

toys. *See* doll and toy projects

transferring designs, 9, 64, 69. *See also* Art Deco Flowers Handbag; Birdie Album Cover

T-shirt project, 23, 42. *See also Woolly Critter T-shirt*

W

wallet. *See* Woolly Wallet

wet felting, 7

wire, 11, 88, 109. *See also* Cute and Cuddly Creatures; Fun Fruit

Wispy Pillow, 54-56
  materials, 55
  template, 118
  variation, 57

Wool and Tulle Winter Hat, 36-37
  fun ideas, 37
  materials, 36

wool batting, 11, 51

wool felt, 9

wool roving, 7, 8. *See also specific projects; Corriedale wool roving; materials, needle felting; Merino wool; Romney wool* roving
  online resources, 124

wool stuffing, 11, 108. *See also* Fun Fruit

Woolly Bangle Bracelet, 23, 26-29
  materials, 27

Woolly Critter T-shirt, 23, 42-43

fun ideas, 43

Woolly Wallet, 47, 72-75
  embellishments, 74, 75
  fun ideas, 75
  materials, 73

Woven wool fabrics, 9

Y

yarn, 16, 45, 56, 65, 74, 97-99, 114-115. *See also* Birdie Album Cover; Birdie Mobile; Free-Form Rose Scarf; Miss Penelope Poppet; Wispy Pillow; Woolly Wallet
  online resources, 124

Check out these other fabulous North Light books!

Warm Fuzzies
Betz White

Warm Fuzzies is filled with techniques, tips and patterns for creating 30 cute and colorful felted projects, including cozy pillows and throws as well as comfortable hats, scarves, pincushions and handbags. Author Betz White will show you how to felt thrift store and bargain sweaters, then cut them up and use them to make quick, adorable projects for the whole family. Learn how to select the best knitted wool for felting, the best way to full it, and how to combine this process with a wide variety of other techniques, including appliqué, knitted I-cord, basic embroidery, needle felting, pre-felting manipulation and more.
ISBN-13: 978-1-60061-007-3
ISBN-10: 1-60061-007-2
paperback 144 pages
Z1026

Nuno Nouveau
Liz Clay

In this unique collection of nuno felt projects, the author inspires the reader with innovative ideas for combining beautiful woven fabrics with handmade felt. The author gives clear instructions about how the nuno process works and demonstrates how it can be used on various fabrics and fibers to create very different results. Each of these techniques is fully illustrated with detailed photographs and clear step-by-step instructions.
ISBN-13: 978-1-60061-036-3
ISBN-10: 1-60061-036-6
paperback 128 pages
Z1379

Soft + Simple Knits for Little Ones
Heidi Boyd

Learn to knit simple, adorable projects for the little ones in your life using the basic techniques taught in this book. *Soft + Simple Knits for Little Ones* includes patterns for clothing, accessories and toys that can be knit for last-minute gifts or for nearly instant gratification. Even if you've never picked up a set of knitting needles, author Heidi Boyd will teach you the skills needed to quickly and successfully complete each of the projects in this book without spending too much money or too much time.
ISBN-13: 978-1-58180-965-7
ISBN-10: 1-58180-965-4
paperback with flaps 160 pages
Z0696

Knitted and Felted Toys
Zoë Halstead

This beautiful collection of 26 delightful toys includes everything from cute and cuddly animals such as a penguin or a lion to well-loved characters, such as a pirate, a mermaid and a princess. With easy-to-follow patterns that use both knitting and felted knitting, there is something for every skill level.
ISBN-13: 978-0-89689-587-4
ISBN-10: 0-89689-587-4
paperback 128 pages
Z1438

These books and other fine North Light books are available at your local craft retailer, bookstore or from online suppliers.